SPANISH
VISUAL DICTIONARY

Published by Collins
An imprint of HarperCollins Publishers
Westerhill Road
Bishopbriggs
Glasgow G64 2QT

First Edition 2019

10 9 8 7 6 5 4 3 2 1

© HarperCollins Publishers 2019

ISBN 978-0-00-829032-0

Collins® is a registered trademark of
HarperCollins Publishers Limited

Typeset by Jouve, India

Printed in China by RR Donnelley APS

Acknowledgements
We would like to thank those authors and
publishers who kindly gave permission for
copyright material to be used in the Collins
Corpus. We would also like to thank Times
Newspapers Ltd for providing valuable data.

All rights reserved. No part of this book may
be reproduced, stored in a retrieval system,
or transmitted in any form or by any means,
electronic, mechanical, photocopying,
recording or otherwise, without the prior
permission in writing of the Publisher.
This book is sold subject to the conditions
that it shall not, by way of trade or otherwise,
be lent, re-sold, hired out or otherwise
circulated without the Publisher's prior consent
in any form of binding or cover other than that
in which it is published and without a similar
condition including this condition being
imposed on the subsequent purchaser.

Entered words that we have reason to believe
constitute trademarks have been designated
as such. However, neither the presence nor
absence of such designation should be regarded
as affecting the legal status of any trademark.

HarperCollins does not warrant that any
website mentioned in this title will be provided
uninterrupted, than any website will be error
free, that defects will be corrected, or that the
website or the server that makes it available
are free of viruses or bugs. For full terms and
conditions please refer to the site terms
provided on the website.

A catalogue record for this book is available
from the British Library

If you would like to comment on any aspect
of this book, please contact us at the given
address or online.
E-mail dictionaries@harpercollins.co.uk
www.facebook.com/collinsdictionary
@collinsdict

MANAGING EDITOR
Maree Airlie

FOR THE PUBLISHER
Gerry Breslin
Gina Macleod
Kevin Robbins
Robin Scrimgeour

CONTRIBUTORS
Ana Cristina Llompart Lucas
Lauren Reid

TECHNICAL SUPPORT
Claire Dimeo

MIX
Paper from
responsible sources
FSC™ C007454

This book is produced from independently certified FSC™ paper
to ensure responsible forest management.

For more information visit: www.harpercollins.co.uk/green

CONTENTS

4 INTRODUCTION

7 **THE ESSENTIALS**

17 **TRANSPORT**

45 **IN THE HOME**

69 **AT THE SHOPS**

113 **DAY-TO-DAY**

141 **LEISURE**

167 **SPORT**

191 **HEALTH**

217 **PLANET EARTH**

237 **CELEBRATIONS AND FESTIVALS**

245 **INDEX**

INTRODUCTION

Whether you're on holiday or staying in a Spanish-speaking country for a slightly longer period of time, your **Collins Visual Dictionary** is designed to help you find exactly what you need, when you need it. With over a thousand clear and helpful images, you can quickly locate the vocabulary you are looking for.

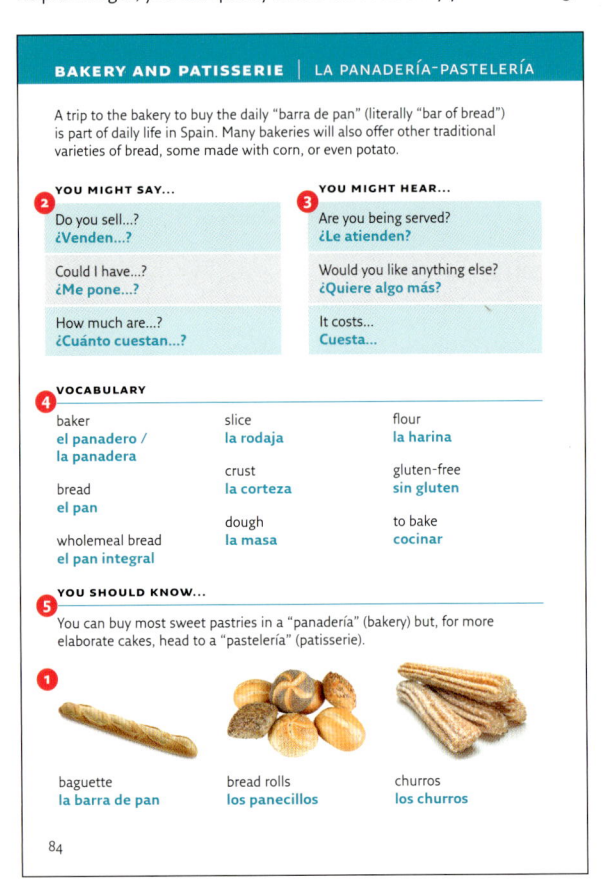

BAKERY AND PATISSERIE | LA PANADERÍA-PASTELERÍA

A trip to the bakery to buy the daily "barra de pan" (literally "bar of bread") is part of daily life in Spain. Many bakeries will also offer other traditional varieties of bread, some made with corn, or even potato.

YOU MIGHT SAY...

Do you sell...?
¿Venden...?

Could I have...?
¿Me pone...?

How much are...?
¿Cuánto cuestan...?

YOU MIGHT HEAR...

Are you being served?
¿Le atienden?

Would you like anything else?
¿Quiere algo más?

It costs...
Cuesta...

VOCABULARY

baker el panadero / la panadera	slice la rodaja	flour la harina
bread el pan	crust la corteza	gluten-free sin gluten
wholemeal bread el pan integral	dough la masa	to bake cocinar

YOU SHOULD KNOW...

You can buy most sweet pastries in a "panadería" (bakery) but, for more elaborate cakes, head to a "pastelería" (patisserie).

baguette
la barra de pan

bread rolls
los panecillos

churros
los churros

84

The Visual Dictionary includes:

- 10 **chapters** arranged thematically, so that you can easily find what you need to suit the situation
- **(1)** **images** – illustrating essential items
- **(2)** **YOU MIGHT SAY...** – common phrases that you might want to use
- **(3)** **YOU MIGHT HEAR...** – common phrases that you might come across
- **(4)** **VOCABULARY** – common words that you might need
- **(5)** **YOU SHOULD KNOW...** – tips about local customs or etiquette
- an **index** to find all images quickly and easily
- essential **phrases** and **numbers** listed on the flaps for quick reference

USING YOUR COLLINS VISUAL DICTIONARY

In order to make sure that the phrases and vocabulary in the **Collins Visual Dictionary** are presented in a way that's clear and easy to understand, we have followed certain policies when translating:

1) In Spain, "tú" can be used for anyone you are on first-name terms with, as well as when talking to children and young people. It is also generally considered appropriate to use "tú" in shops, banks and so on to address the people working there, particularly if they are young. However, it is best avoided when addressing people in authority or older strangers, unless you are invited to use "tú", for instance:

    Shall we call each other "tú"? **¿Nos tuteamos?**

    In this dictionary, we have used either "tú" or "usted" depending on what was deemed to be more likely in a given context, for example:

    When is your birthday? **¿Cuándo es tu cumpleaños?** (informal)
    May I ask how old you are? **¿Puedo preguntarle qué edad tiene?** (formal)

2) The grammatical gender of Spanish nouns has been indicated using the articles "el" (masculine singular), "la" (feminine singular), "los" (masculine plural) and "las" (feminine plural).

    key **la llave**
    building **el edificio**
    curtains **las cortinas**
    shoes los **zapatos**

    When a feminine word in Spanish starts with stressed "a", it takes the masculine article, rather than the feminine, to make it easier to pronounce.

These have been marked with the label *f* to indicate that it is a feminine word even if preceded by the masculine article "el":

    water **el agua** *f*
    eagle **el águila** *f*

When a Spanish noun has both a masculine and feminine form (as in the case of many professions), both forms are shown:

    nurse **el enfermero / la enfermera**

3) The masculine form of adjectives only has been shown for vocabulary items and in phrases, for example:

    happy **contento**
    I'm tired. **Estoy cansado.**

Remember that, in Spanish, the adjective often changes depending on whether the noun it describes is masculine or feminine. Often the ending of the adjective changes from "o" to "a", so "cansado" becomes "cansada", although there are some adjective endings that behave differently.

Plural forms of both adjectives and nouns are generally formed by adding "-s" or "-es" to the end of the word:

    The girls are tired. **Las niñas están cansadas.**

However, some words, among them the days of the week, are the same in both singular and plural:

    the umbrella **el paraguas**
    the umbrellas **los paraguas**
    I'm busy next Monday **Estoy ocupado el próximo lunes.**
    I'm always busy on Mondays. **Siempre estoy ocupado los lunes.**

When an adjective or noun ends in "-z", the plural form becomes "-ces":

    feliz => *pl* **felices**

FREE AUDIO

We have created a free audio resource to help you learn and practise the Spanish words for all of the images shown in this dictionary. The Spanish words in each chapter are spoken by native speakers, giving you the opportunity to listen to each word twice and repeat it yourself. Download the audio from the website below to learn all of the vocabulary you need for communicating in Spanish.

www.collins.co.uk/visualdictionary

THE ESSENTIALS | LO ESENCIAL

Whether you're going to be visiting a Spanish-speaking country, or even living there, you'll want to be able to chat with people and get to know them better. Being able to communicate effectively with acquaintances, friends, family, and colleagues is key to becoming more confident in Spanish in a variety of everyday situations.

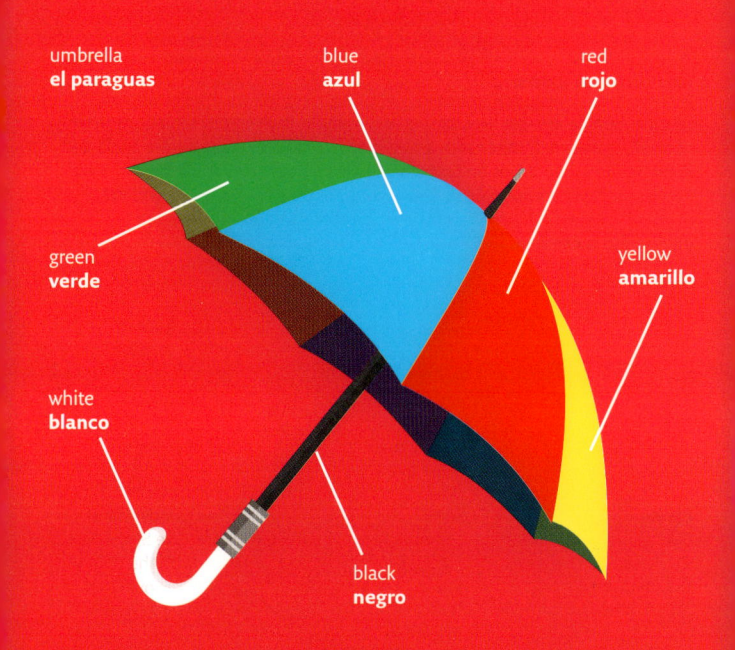

umbrella
el paraguas

blue
azul

red
rojo

green
verde

yellow
amarillo

white
blanco

black
negro

THE BASICS | LO ESENCIAL

Hello/Hi!
¡Hola!

Good morning.
Buenos días.

Good afternoon.
Buenas tardes.

Good evening.
Buenas tardes / noches.

Goodnight.
Buenas noches.

See you soon.
Hasta pronto.

See you later.
Hasta luego.

See you tomorrow.
Hasta mañana.

See you on Saturday.
Hasta el sábado.

Bye!
¡Adiós!

Have a good day/evening!
¡Que pases un buen día! / una buena noche!

Pleased to meet you.
Encantado.

YOU SHOULD KNOW…

Spanish people are very welcoming and friendly. In everyday situations, men normally greet each other with a hug, a handshake, or a pat on the back, and greet women with a kiss on both cheeks; women also greet each other with two kisses. In more formal situations, a handshake is fine, and if you are meeting for the first time, it is polite to say "Encantado / Encantada" (Pleased to meet you).

Yes.
Sí.

No.
No.

I don't know.
No sé.

Please.
Por favor.

Yes, please.
Sí, por favor.

Thank you.
Gracias.

No, thanks.
No, gracias.

Excuse me.
Perdone.

Sorry?
¿Perdón?

I'm sorry.
Lo siento.

OK!
¡De acuerdo!

You're welcome.
De nada.

I don't understand.
No entiendo.

ABOUT YOU | SOBRE TÍ

How old are you?
¿Cuántos años tienes?

May I ask how old you are?
¿Puedo preguntarle qué edad tiene?

When is your birthday?
¿Cuándo es tu cumpleaños?

I'm ... years old.
Tengo ... años.

My birthday is on...
Mi cumpleaños es el...

I was born in...
Nací el...

Where are you from?
¿De dónde eres?

Where do you live?
¿Dónde vives?

I live in...
Vivo en...

I'm from...
Soy de...

... the UK.
... el Reino Unido.

I'm...
Soy...

Scottish
escocés

English
inglés

Irish
irlandés

Welsh
galés

British
británico

Are you married/single?
(to a man)
¿Estás casado / soltero?

Are you married/single?
(to a woman)
¿Estás casada / soltera?

I'm married/single. (man)
Estoy casado / soltero.

I'm married/single. (woman)
Estoy casada / soltera.

I have a partner.
Tengo pareja.

I'm divorced/widowed. (man)
Estoy divorciado / viudo.

I'm divorced/widowed. (woman)
Estoy divorciada / viuda.

Do you have any children?
¿Tienes hijos?

I have ... children.
Tengo ... hijos.

I don't have any children.
No tengo hijos.

FAMILY AND FRIENDS | LA FAMILIA Y LOS AMIGOS

This is my...
Este / Esta es mi...

These are my...
Estos / Estas son mis...

This is my wife.
Esta es mi mujer.

These are my parents.
Estos son mis padres.

husband
el marido

wife
la mujer

son
el hijo

daughter
la hija

child
el niño / la niña

partner
la pareja

boyfriend
el novio

girlfriend
la novia

fiancé/fiancée
el prometido / la prometida

father
el padre

mother
la madre

brother
el hermano

sister
la hermana

grandfather
el abuelo

grandmother
la abuela

grandson
el nieto

granddaughter
la nieta

father-in-law
el suegro

mother-in-law
la suegra

daughter-in-law
la nuera

son-in-law
el yerno

brother-in-law
el cuñado

sister-in-law
la cuñada

stepfather
el padrastro

stepmother
la madrastra

stepson
el hijastro

stepdaughter
la hijastra

step-/half-brother
el hermanastro

step-/half-sister
la hermanastra

uncle
el tío

aunt
la tía

nephew
el sobrino

niece
la sobrina

cousin
el primo / la prima

friend
el amigo / la amiga

neighbour
el vecino / la vecina

GENERAL HEALTH AND WELLBEING | SALUD Y BIENESTAR

How are you?
¿Cómo estás?

How's it going?
¿Qué tal?

How is he/she?
¿Cómo está (él / ella)?

How are they?
¿Cómo están?

Very well, thanks, and you?
Muy bien, gracias. ¿Y tú?

Fine, thanks.
Bien, gracias.

Great!
¡Fenomenal!

So-so.
Así, así.

Not bad, thanks.
Bastante bien, gracias.

Could be worse.
Voy tirando.

Awful.
Fatal.

I'm fine.
Estoy bien.

I'm tired.
Estoy cansado.

I'm hungry/thirsty.
Tengo hambre / sed.

I'm full.
Estoy lleno.

I'm cold.
Tengo frío.

I'm warm.
Tengo calor.

I am...
Estoy...

He/She is...
Está...

They are...
Están...

happy
contento

excited
entusiasmado

surprised
sorprendido

annoyed
enfadado

angry
enfadado

sad
triste

worried
preocupado

depressed
deprimido

bored
aburrido

I'm afraid.
Tengo miedo.

I feel...
Me siento...

He/She feels...
Se siente...

They feel...
Se sienten...

well
bien

unwell
mal

better
mejor

worse
peor

WORK | EL TRABAJO

Where do you work?
¿Dónde trabajas?

What do you do?
¿A qué te dedicas?

What's your occupation?
¿Cuál es tu ocupación?

Do you work/study?
¿Trabajas / Estudias?

I'm self-employed.
Soy autónomo / autónoma.

I'm unemployed.
Estoy en paro.

I'm at university.
Estoy en la universidad.

I'm retired.
Estoy jubilado.

I'm travelling.
Me dedico a viajar.

I work from home.
Trabajo desde casa.

I work part-/full-time.
Trabajo a tiempo parcial / completo.

I work as a/an...
Trabajo de...

I'm a/an...
Soy...

I'm a shop assistant.
Soy dependiente.

My sister is an engineer.
Mi hermana es ingeniera.

builder
el albañil / la albañil

chef
el chef / la chef

civil servant
el funcionario / la funcionaria

cleaner
el limpiador / la limpiadora

cook
el cocinero / la cocinera

dentist
el dentista / la dentista

doctor
el médico / la médica

driver
el conductor / la conductora

electrician
el electricista / la electricista

engineer
el ingeniero / la ingeniera

farmer
el agricultor / la agricultora

firefighter
el bombero / la bombero

fisherman
el pescador / la pescadora

IT worker
el informático / la informática

joiner
el carpintero / la carpintera

journalist
el periodista / la periodista

lawyer
el abogado / la abogada

mechanic
el mecánico / la mecánica

nurse
el enfermero / la enfermera

office worker
el oficinista / la oficinista

plumber
el fontanero / la fontanera

police officer
el agente de policía / la agente de policía

postal worker
el cartero / la cartera

primary school teacher
el maestro / la maestra

sailor
el marinero / la marinera

salesperson
el vendedor / la vendedora

scientist
el científico / la científica

secondary school teacher
el profesor / la profesora

soldier
el soldado / la soldado

vet
el veterinario / la veterinaria

waiter
el camarero

waitress
la camarera

I work at/in...
Trabajo en...

business
el negocio

company
la empresa

construction site
la obra

factory
la fábrica

government
el gobierno

hospital
el hospital

hotel
el hotel

office
la oficina

restaurant
el restaurante

school
el colegio

shop
la tienda

TIME | LA HORA

morning	**la mañana**
afternoon	**la tarde**
evening	**la noche**
night	**la noche**
midday	**el mediodía**
midnight	**la medianoche**
today	**hoy**
tonight	**esta noche**
tomorrow	**mañana**
yesterday	**ayer**
What time is it?	**¿Qué hora es?**
It's nine o'clock.	**Son las nueve.**
It's ten past nine.	**Son las nueve y diez.**
It's quarter past nine.	**Son las nueve y cuarto.**
It's half past nine.	**Son las nueve y media.**
It's 20 to ten.	**Son las diez menos veinte.**
It's quarter to ten.	**Son las diez menos cuarto.**
It's 10 a.m.	**Son las diez (de la mañana).**
It's 5 p.m.	**Son las cinco (de la tarde).**
It's 17:30.	**Son las diecisiete treinta.**
When...?	**¿Cuándo...?**
... in 60 seconds/two minutes.	**... dentro de 60 segundos / dos minutos.**
... in an hour/quarter of an hour.	**... dentro de una hora / un cuarto de hora.**
... in half an hour.	**... dentro de media hora.**
early	**temprano**
late	**tarde**
soon	**pronto**
later	**más tarde**
now	**ahora**

YOU SHOULD KNOW...

Spaniards tend to think about the time of day slightly differently to the British. "La mañana" (morning) could be anything up till around 1 p.m., and lunchtime (around 1.30-3.00 p.m.) is called "mediodía" (midday). "La tarde" can encompass both afternoon and evening (roughly between 3-8 p.m.).

DAYS, MONTHS, AND SEASONS
LOS DÍAS, LOS MESES Y LAS ESTACIONES

Monday **el lunes**	Wednesday **el miércoles**	Friday **el viernes**	Sunday **el domingo**
Tuesday **el martes**	Thursday **el jueves**	Saturday **el sábado**	

January **enero**	April **abril**	July **julio**	October **octubre**
February **febrero**	May **mayo**	August **agosto**	November **noviembre**
March **marzo**	June **junio**	September **septiembre**	December **diciembre**

day
el día

weekend
el fin de semana

week
la semana

fortnight
la quincena

month
el mes

year
el año

decade
la década

daily
diario

weekly
semanal

fortnightly
quincenal

monthly
mensual

yearly
anual

on Mondays
los lunes

every Sunday
todos los domingos

last Thursday
el jueves pasado

next Friday
el próximo viernes

the week before/after
la semana anterior / después

in February
en febrero

in 2019
en 2019

in the '80s
en la década de los ochenta

spring
la primavera

summer
el verano

autumn
la otoño

winter
el invierno

in spring/winter
en primavera / invierno

THE WEATHER | EL TIEMPO

How's the weather?
¿Qué tiempo hace?

What's the forecast for today/tomorrow?
¿Cuál es el pronóstico del tiempo para hoy / mañana?

How warm/cold is it?
¿Hace calor / frío?

Is it going to rain?
¿Va a llover?

What a lovely day!
¡Qué tiempo tan bueno!

What awful weather!
¡Qué tiempo tan horrible!

It's sunny/windy.
Hace sol / viento.

It's warm/hot.
Hace calorcito / calor.

It's cloudy.
Está nublado.

It's misty/foggy.
Hay neblina / niebla.

It's freezing.
Hace mucho frío.

It's raining.
Llueve.

It's wet.
Está lluvioso.

It's snowing.
Nieva.

It's humid.
Hay mucha humedad.

It's stormy.
Hay tormenta.

It's changeable.
Está muy variable.

nice
bueno

horrible
malo

cool
fresco

mild
suave

temperature
la temperatura

sun
el sol

rain
la lluvia

snow
la nieve

hail
el granizo

wind
el viento

gale
el vendaval

mist
la neblina

fog
la niebla

thunder
el trueno

lightning
el relámpago

thunderstorm
la tormenta

cloud
la nube

TRANSPORT | LOS MEDIOS DE TRANSPORTE

Travelling to Spain from the UK is easier than ever before, with many regular flights to numerous Spanish destinations. The same can be said of travelling around Spain - there is a good railway system (it can be quicker to travel by train than by plane between certain cities). The country is well connected by road, and local public transport is widely developed with good tram, bus, and metro systems in larger cities such as Madrid and Barcelona.

helicopter
el helicóptero

rotor
el rotor

blade
la paleta

cockpit
la cabina del piloto

nose
el morro

tail
la cola

THE BASICS | LO ESENCIAL

When asking for directions, it's easiest simply to state your destination, followed by "por favor". It's always most polite to use "Señor" or "Señora" to address any passers-by you stop and ask.

YOU MIGHT SAY...

Excuse me...
Perdone...

Where is...?
¿Dónde está...?

Which way is...?
¿Cómo se va a / al / a la...?

What's the quickest way to...?
¿Cuál es el camino más rápido para...?

How far away is it?
¿A qué distancia está?

Is it far from here?
¿Está lejos de aquí?

I'm lost.
Estoy perdido.

I'm looking for...
Busco...

I'm going...
Voy...

Can I walk there?
¿Puedo ir hasta allí a pie?

I'd like a taxi to...
Quería un taxi a...

YOU MIGHT HEAR...

It's over there.
Está ahí.

It's in the other direction.
Está en la otra dirección.

It's ... metres/minutes from here.
Está a ... metros / minutos de aquí.

Go straight ahead.
Siga todo recto.

Turn left/right.
Gire a la izquierda / derecha.

It's next to...
Está junto a...

It's opposite...
Está frente a...

It's near to...
Está cerca de...

Follow the signs for...
Siga las señales para...

VOCABULARY

street
la calle

driver
**el conductor /
la conductora**

passenger
**el pasajero /
la pasajera**

pedestrian
**el peatón /
la peatona**

traffic
el tráfico

traffic jam
el embotellamiento

rush hour
la hora punta

public transport
el transporte público

taxi
el taxi

taxi rank
la parada de taxis

season ticket
**el abono de
transporte**

travel card
**la tarjeta de
transporte**

directions
las señas

GPS
el GPS

mapping app
**la aplicación de
mapas**

road sign
la señal de carretera

route
la ruta

special assistance
la asistencia

to walk
caminar

to drive
conducir

to return
regresar

to cross
cruzar

to turn
girar

YOU SHOULD KNOW...

Season tickets ("el abono de transporte") that can be used across different forms of public transport are very commonly used in metropolitan areas in Spain.

map
el mapa

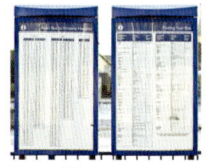

ticket
el billete

timetable
el horario

CAR | EL COCHE

Traffic drives on the right-hand side in Spain. Remember to carry your ID, driving licence, proof of insurance, and car registration documents with you while driving in Spain.

YOU MIGHT SAY...

Is this the road to...?
¿Es esta la carretera a...?

Can I park here?
¿Puedo aparcar aquí?

Do I have to pay to park?
¿Tengo que pagar por aparcar?

Where can I hire a car?
¿Dónde puedo alquilar un coche?

I'd like to hire a car...
Quería alquilar un coche...

... for four days/a week.
... para cuatro días / una semana.

What is your daily rate?
¿Cuál es el precio por día?

When/Where must I return it?
¿Cuándo / Dónde debo devolverlo?

Where is the nearest petrol station?
¿Dónde está la gasolinera más cercana?

I've put in ... litres/euros of petrol.
He puesto ... litros / euros de gasolina.

YOU MIGHT HEAR...

You can/can't park here.
Puede / No puede aparcar aquí.

It's free to park here.
El aparcamiento es gratuito aquí.

It costs ... to park here.
Aparcar aquí cuesta...

Car hire is ... per day/week.
El alquiler del coche es ... por día / por semana.

May I see your documents, please?
¿Puedo ver sus documentos, por favor?

Please return it to...
Por favor, devuélvalo en...

Please return the car with a full tank of fuel.
Por favor, devuelva el coche con el depósito lleno.

Which pump are you at?
¿En qué surtidor está aparcado?

VOCABULARY

people carrier
el monovolumen

motorhome
la autocaravana

caravan
la caravana

passenger seat
el asiento del copiloto

driver's seat
el asiento del conductor

back seat
el asiento trasero

child seat
la silla infantil

roof rack
la baca

sunroof
el techo solar

automatic
automático

electric
eléctrico

hybrid
híbrido

engine
el motor

battery
la batería

brake
el freno

accelerator
el acelerador

air conditioning
el aire acondicionado

clutch
el embrague

cruise control
el control de crucero

exhaust (pipe)
el tubo de escape

fuel tank
el depósito de gasolina

gearbox
la caja de cambios

transmission
la trasmisión

Breathalyser®
el alcoholímetro

to start the engine
poner el motor en marcha

to brake
frenar

to overtake
adelantar

to park
aparcar

to reverse
dar marcha atrás

to slow down
aminorar la velocidad

to speed
conducir a exceso de velocidad

to stop
parar

YOU SHOULD KNOW...

Radar warning systems that have been built into sat navs can be used in Spain. However, devices that can physically detect or interfere with speed cameras are illegal.

EXTERIOR

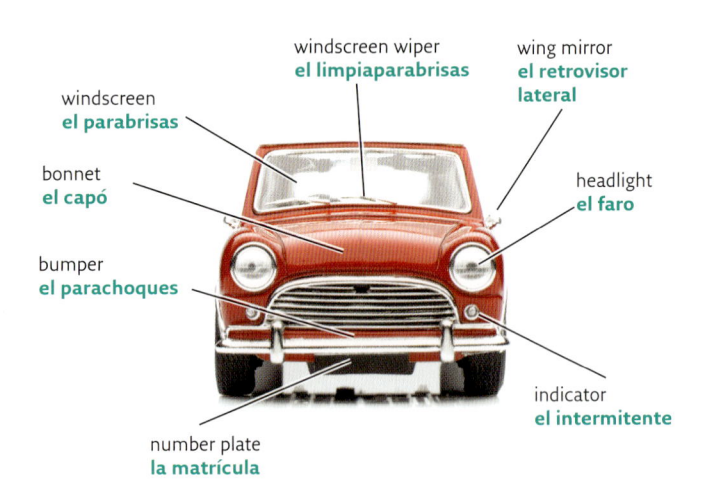

boot
el maletero

roof
el techo

window
la ventanilla

wheel
la rueda

door
la puerta

wing
la aleta

tyre
el neumático

windscreen wiper
el limpiaparabrisas

wing mirror
el retrovisor lateral

windscreen
el parabrisas

bonnet
el capó

headlight
el faro

bumper
el parachoques

indicator
el intermitente

number plate
la matrícula

INTERIOR

dashboard
el salpicadero

fuel gauge
el indicador de la gasolina

gearstick
la palanca de marchas

glove compartment
la guantera

handbrake
el freno de mano

headrest
el reposacabezas

ignition
el encendido

rearview mirror
el retrovisor

sat nav
el sistema de navegación

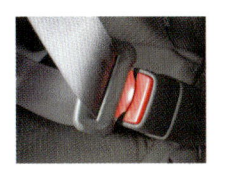

seatbelt
el cinturón de seguridad

speedometer
el velocímetro

steering wheel
el volante

DRIVING | LA CONDUCCIÓN

Spain has an excellent motorway system, but be aware that some "autopistas" (motorways) are toll-paying. Where possible, avoid motorway travel during "el éxodo vacacional" (the holiday exodus) – periods of dense road traffic that occur at the beginning of Spanish holiday times.

VOCABULARY

dual carriageway
la autovía

single-track road
la carretera de un solo carril

tarmac®
el asfalto

corner
la esquina

exit
la salida

slip road
la vía de acceso

layby
el área de descanso *f*

speed limit
la velocidad máxima

diversion
el desvío

driving licence
el permiso de conducir

car registration document
el permiso de circulación

car insurance
el seguro de automóvil

traffic fine
la multa de tráfico

car hire/rental
el alquiler de coches

car sharing scheme
el sistema de carsharing

residents' parking
la zona verde

pay-and-display
la zona azul

ticket machine
la máquina expendedora de billetes

unleaded petrol
la gasolina sin plomo

diesel
el gasóleo

roadworks
las obras de carretera

YOU SHOULD KNOW...

Speed limits on Spanish roads go by kmph, not mph. The speed limits are 50 kmph (31 mph) for built-up areas, 90 kmph (56 mph) on two-lane highways, 100 kmph (62 mph) on dual carriageways, and 120 kmph (75 mph) on motorways.

accessible parking space
la plaza de aparcamiento accesible

bridge
el puente

car park
el parking

car wash
el lavachoches

fuel pump
el surtidor de gasolina

junction
el cruce

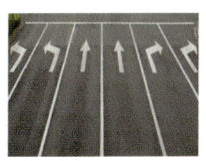

kerb
el bordillo

lane
el carril

level crossing
el paso a nivel

motorway
la autopista

parking meter
el parquímetro

parking space
la plaza de aparcamiento

pavement
la acera

petrol station
la gasolinera

pothole
el bache

road
la carretera

roundabout
la rotonda

speed camera
el radar de velocidad

toll point
la estación de peaje

traffic cone
el cono de tráfico

traffic lights
el semáforo

traffic warden
**el guardia de tráfico /
la guardia de tráfico**

tunnel
el túnel

zebra crossing
el paso de cebra

CAR TROUBLE | PROBLEMAS CON EL COCHE

If you break down on the motorway, call the police or the breakdown service operating in that area using one of the orange emergency telephones that are located every 2 km along the side of the road. Otherwise, call 112 to contact the emergency services.

YOU MIGHT SAY...

Can you help me?
¿Puede ayudarme?

I've broken down.
Se me ha estropeado el coche.

I've had an accident.
He tenido un accidente.

I've run out of petrol.
Me he quedado sin gasolina.

I've got a flat tyre.
Se me ha pinchado una rueda.

I've lost my car keys.
He perdido las llaves del coche.

The car won't start.
El coche no arranca.

There's a problem with...
Hay un problema con...

I've been injured.
Estoy herido.

Call an ambulance.
Llame a una ambulancia.

Can you send a breakdown van?
¿Puede enviarme una grúa?

Is there a garage/petrol station nearby?
¿Hay un garaje / una gasolinera cerca de aquí?

Can you tow me to a garage?
¿Puede remolcarme hasta un garaje?

Can you help me change this wheel?
¿Puede ayudarme a cambiar la rueda?

How much will a repair cost?
¿Cuánto costará la reparación?

When will the car be fixed?
¿Cuándo estará arreglado el coche?

May I take your insurance details?
¿Podría darme los datos de su seguro?

YOU MIGHT HEAR...

Do you need any help?
¿Puedo ayudarle?

Are you hurt?
¿Está herido?

What's wrong with your car?
¿Qué problema tiene su coche?

Where have you broken down?
¿Dónde se le ha averiado el coche?

I can tow you to...
Puedo remolcarle hasta...

I can give you a jumpstart.
Puedo ponerle en marcha el motor con los cables de arranque.

The repairs will cost...
La reparación le costará...

We need to order new parts.
Necesitamos pedir repuestos.

The car will be ready by Monday.
El coche estará listo para el lunes.

I need your insurance details.
Necesito los datos de su seguro.

Call an ambulance/the police!
¡Llame a una ambulancia / a la policía!

VOCABULARY

accident
el accidente

breakdown
la avería

collision
la colisión

flat tyre
el pinchazo

to break down
averiarse

to have an accident
tener un accidente

to have a flat tyre
tener un pinchazo

to change a tyre
cambiar una rueda

to tow
remolcar

YOU SHOULD KNOW...

When driving a British-registered car in Spain, you are legally required to have the following in your car: headlight converters; spare bulbs and fuses; warning triangles; hi-viz vests; a spare wheel; and tools for a tyre change. If you are driving a UK-registered vehicle, you must also display a GB sticker plate at the rear of the car or have registration plates with the GB Euro symbol.

airbag **el airbag**	antifreeze **el anticongelante**	emergency phone **el poste SOS**
garage **el garaje**	hi-viz vest **el chaleco reflectante**	jack **el gato**
jump leads **los cables de arranque**	mechanic **el mecánico / la mecánica**	snow chains **las cadenas para nieve**
spare wheel **la rueda de recambio**	tow truck **la grúa**	warning triangle **el triángulo de emergencia**

BUS | EL AUTOBÚS

Local bus services are often well organized and frequent; for longer journeys, rail services are usually faster than bus or coach services.

YOU MIGHT SAY...

Is there a bus to...?
¿Hay un autobús a...?

When is the next bus to...?
¿A qué hora sale el próximo autobús a...?

Which bus goes to the city centre?
¿Qué autobús va al centro de la ciudad?

Where is the bus stop?
¿Dónde está la parada del autobús?

Which stand does the coach leave from?
¿De qué dársena sale el autocar?

Where can I buy tickets?
¿Dónde puedo comprar los billetes?

How much is it to go to...?
¿Cuánto cuesta ir a...?

A young person/An over 60/ A group fare, please.
Un billete de tarifa joven / para mayores de 60 / para grupo, por favor.

A single/return ticket, please.
Un billete sencillo / de ida y vuelta, por favor.

Could you tell me when to get off?
¿Podría decirme dónde bajarme?

How many stops is it?
¿Cuántas paradas son?

I want to get off at the next stop, please.
Quiero bajarme en la próxima parada, por favor.

YOU MIGHT HEAR...

The number 17 goes to...
La línea / El número 17 va a...

The bus stop is down the road.
El autobús para al final de la calle.

It leaves from stand 21.
Sale de la dársena 21.

There's a bus every 10 minutes.
Hay un autobús cada 10 minutos.

You buy tickets at the machine.
Puede comprar los billetes en la máquina.

This is your stop, sir/madam.
Esta es su parada, señor / señora.

VOCABULARY

bus route
la ruta del autobús

bus lane
el carril del autobús

bus station
la estación de autobuses

bus pass
el abono de autobús

ticket inspector
**el revisor /
la revisora**

fare
el billete

reduced fare
la tarifa con descuento

card reader
el lector de tarjetas

wheelchair access
el acceso para silla de ruedas

night bus
el autobús nocturno

shuttle bus
la lanzadera

school bus
el autobús escolar

tour bus
el autobús de excursión

to catch the bus
tomar el autobús

to tap/swipe your card
tocar el lector con el billete

YOU SHOULD KNOW...

When travelling by bus in the city, you have to "validar el billete" (to validate the ticket) by tapping your travel card on the reader or inserting your ticket in the machine.

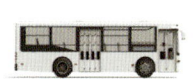

bus
el autobús

bus shelter
la marquesina

bus stop
la parada de autobús

coach
el autocar

minibus
el microbús

sightseeing bus
el autobús turístico

BICYCLE | LA BICICLETA

Spain is part of the Eurovelo network, and also has a series of routes for cyclists: "Carriles bici" are cycle lanes that run parallel to roads; "sendas ciclables" are cycling routes that do not follow main roads; and "aceras bici" are urban cycle paths. Many towns and cities have public bike rental schemes.

YOU MIGHT SAY...

Where can I hire a bicycle?
¿Dónde puedo alquilar una bicicleta?

How much is it to hire?
¿Cuánto cuesta alquilarla?

My bike has a puncture.
Mi bicicleta tiene una rueda pinchada.

Is there a cycle path nearby?
¿Hay una senda ciclable cerca?

YOU MIGHT HEAR...

Bike hire is ... per day/week.
El alquiler de la bici es ... por día / por semana.

You must wear a helmet.
Tiene que usar un casco protector.

There's a cycle lane from ... to...
Hay un carril bici que va desde ... a...

There is a public bike hire scheme here.
Hay un servicio de bicicletas públicas aquí.

VOCABULARY

cyclist
el ciclista / la ciclista

mountain bike
la bicicleta de montaña

road bike
la bicicleta de carretera

tandem
el tándem

bike stand
el soporte para bici

bike rack
el aparcabicis

child seat
la silla portabebé

cycle path
el carril bici

puncture repair kit
el kit de reparación de neumáticos

reflective vest
el chalecho reflectante

cycling shorts
el culotte de ciclismo

to cycle
ir en bicicleta

to go for a bike ride
ir a dar una vuelta en bici

YOU SHOULD KNOW...

Spain hosts the world-famous cycling road race, the Vuelta a España.

ACCESSORIES

bell
el timbre

bike lock
el candado para la bicicleta

front light
la luz delantera

helmet
el casco

pump
la bomba

reflector
el reflector

BICYCLE

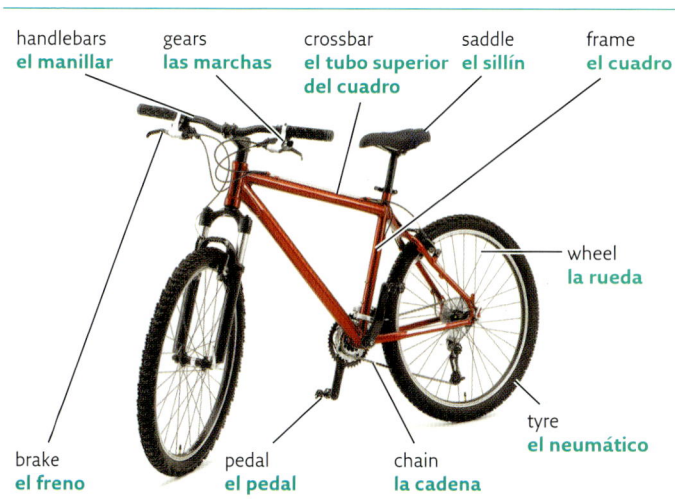

handlebars
el manillar

gears
las marchas

crossbar
el tubo superior del cuadro

saddle
el sillín

frame
el cuadro

wheel
la rueda

tyre
el neumático

brake
el freno

pedal
el pedal

chain
la cadena

MOTORBIKE | LA MOTO

VOCABULARY

motorcyclist
**el motorista /
la motorista**

moped
el ciclomotor

scooter
la motocicleta

fuel tank
el depósito de gasolina

handlebars
el manillar

headlight
el faro

mudguard
el guardabarros

kickstand
la pata

leathers
el traje de cuero

YOU SHOULD KNOW...

Motorcyclists must wear hi-viz clothing and have reflective elements on their helmets.

boots
las botas

helmet
el casco

helmet cam
la cámara para casco

leather gloves
los guantes de cuero

leather jacket
la chaqueta de cuero

motorbike
la moto

RAIL TRAVEL | EL TRANSPORTE EN TREN

Spain has an efficient rail network, with many high-speed trains. On long intercity journeys ("trenes de largo recorrido"), you must have a seat reservation, which you can book online or purchase at the station. There is also a good network of "trenes de cercanías" (suburban trains), many of which are double-deckers.

YOU MIGHT SAY...

Is there a train to...?
¿Hay un tren a...?

When is the next train to...?
¿A qué hora sale el próximo tren a...?

Where is the nearest metro station?
¿Dónde está la estación de metro más próxima?

Which platform does it leave from?
¿De qué andén sale?

Which line do I take for...?
¿Qué línea tomo para...?

A ticket to ..., please.
Un billete para ..., por favor.

I'd like to reserve a seat/couchette, please.
Quería reservar un asiento / una litera.

Do I have to change trains?
¿Tengo que cambiar de tren?

Where do I change for...?
¿Dónde cambio para...?

Where is platform 4?
¿Dónde está el andén número 4?

Is this the right platform for...?
¿Es este el andén correcto para...?

Is this the train for...?
¿Es este el tren para...?

Is this seat free?
¿Está libre este asiento?

Where is the restaurant car?
¿Dónde está el coche restaurante / cafetería?

I've missed my train!
¡He perdido el tren!

YOU SHOULD KNOW...

Most major cities in Spain have an underground system, many of which offer a "tarjeta monedero" (rechargable card) that allows you to travel on the metro, and sometimes on other forms of public transport too.

YOU MIGHT HEAR...

The next train leaves at...
El próximo tren sale a la(s)...

Would you like a single or return ticket?
¿Quiere un billete sencillo o de ida y vuelta?

I'm sorry, this journey is fully booked.
Lo siento, este tren está completo.

You must change at...
Tiene que cambiar de tren en...

Platform 4 is down there.
El andén 4 está ahí delante.

This is the right train/platform.
Este es el tren / el andén correcto.

You have to go to platform 2.
Tiene que ir al andén número 2.

This seat is free/taken/reserved.
Este asiento está libre / ocupado / reservado.

The restaurant car is in coach D.
El coche cafetería está en el vagón D.

There is a trolley service on board.
El tren tiene servicio de bar móvil.

The next stop is...
La próxima parada es...

Change here for...
Cambie aquí para...

Your tickets, please.
Sus billetes, por favor.

VOCABULARY

rail network
la red ferroviaria

high-speed train
el tren de alta velocidad

passenger train
el tren de pasajeros

freight train
el tren de mercancías

sleeper
el trenhotel

coach
el vagón

line
la línea

metro station
la estación de metro

left luggage
la consigna de equipaje

train conductor
le revisor / la revisora

security check
el control de acceso

railcard
la tarjeta de descuento para viajes en tren

single ticket
el billete de ida

return ticket
el billete de ida y vuelta

e-ticket
el billete electrónico

first-class
la primera clase

to change trains
cambiar de tren

season ticket
el abono transporte

quiet coach
el vagón silencioso

to validate a ticket
validar un billete

ticket reader
el lector de billetes

reserved seat
el asiento reservado

carriage
el vagón

couchette
la litera

departure board
la pantalla de información

guard
el jefe de tren / la jefa de tren

light railway
el tren ligero

luggage rack
el portaequipajes

metro
el metro

platform
el andén

refreshments trolley
el bar móvil

restaurant car
el coche restaurante

sliding doors
las puertas corredizas

ticket barrier
el torno

ticket machine
la máquina expendedora de billetes

ticket office
la taquilla

track
la vía de tren

train
el tren

train station
la estación de tren

tram
el tranvía

38

AIR TRAVEL | LOS VIAJES EN AVIÓN

Spain has many airports, but many airlines only operate seasonal routes from the UK to some areas of Spain. It is best to check when flights to less central destinations are available.

YOU MIGHT SAY...

I'm looking for check-in/my gate.
Busco la facturación / mi puerta.

I'm checking in one case.
Voy a facturar una maleta.

Which gate does the plane leave from?
¿De qué puerta sale el avión?

When does the gate open/close?
¿Cuándo comienza / termina el embarque?

Is the flight on time?
¿Sale el avión a la hora?

I've lost my luggage.
He perdido mi equipaje.

My flight has been delayed.
Mi vuelo se ha retrasado.

I've missed my flight.
He perdido mi vuelo.

I've missed my connecting flight.
He perdido mi conexión.

Is there a shuttle bus service?
¿Hay (un servicio de autobús) lanzadera?

YOU MIGHT HEAR...

Check-in has opened for flight...
Se ha abierto la facturación para el vuelo...

May I see your ticket/passport, please?
¿Puedo ver su billete / pasaporte, por favor?

How many bags are you checking in?
¿Cuántas maletas va a facturar?

Please go to gate number...
Por favor, diríjase a la puerta número...

Your flight is on time.
Su vuelo llega / sale a la hora.

Your flight is delayed/cancelled.
Su vuelo está retrasado / se ha cancelado.

Is this your bag?
¿Es esta su maleta?

Flight ... is now ready for boarding.
Vamos a iniciar el embarque del vuelo...

Last call for passenger...
Última llamada para el pasajero...

VOCABULARY

airline
la compañía aérea

terminal
la terminal

Arrivals/Departures
Llegadas / Salidas

self check-in
el mostrador de facturación automática

security
la seguridad

body scanner
el escáner corporal

customs
la aduana

passport control
el control de pasaportes

gate
la puerta de embarque

business/economy class
la clase business / turista

cabin crew
la tripulación

flight attendant
el auxiliar de vuelo / la auxiliar de vuelo

aisle
el pasillo

tray table
la bandeja plegable

overhead locker
el compartimento superior

seatbelt
el cinturón de seguridad

wing
el ala *f*

engine
el motor

fuselage
el fuselaje

hold
la bodega

hold luggage
el equipaje facturado

excess baggage
el exceso de equipaje

hand/cabin baggage
el equipaje de mano / cabina

connecting flight
el vuelo de conexión

jetlag
el desfase horario

to check in (online)
facturar (en línea)

aeroplane
el avión

airport
el aeropuerto

baggage reclaim
la recogida de equipajes

boarding card
la tarjeta de embarque

cabin
la cabina

check-in desk
el mostrador de facturación

cockpit
la cabina del piloto

departure board
la pantalla de información

duty-free shop
la tienda libre de impuestos

holdall
la bolsa de viaje

luggage trolley
el carrito portaequipajes

passport
el pasaporte

pilot
el piloto / la piloto

runway
la pista de aterrizaje

suitcase
la maleta

41

FERRY AND BOAT TRAVEL | LOS VIAJES EN BARCO

There are numerous ports on the northern and southern coasts of Spain, connecting the country to various European and North African destinations.

YOU MIGHT SAY...

When is the next boat to...?
¿Cuándo sale el próximo barco para...?

Where does the boat leave from?
¿De dónde sale el barco?

What time is the last boat to...?
¿A qué hora sale el último barco para...?

How long is the trip/crossing?
¿Cuánto dura el viaje / la travesía?

How many crossings a day are there?
¿Cuántas travesías hay al día?

How much for ... passengers?
¿Cuánto es por ... pasajeros?

How much is it for a vehicle?
¿Cuánto cuesta hacer una reserva para un coche?

I feel seasick.
Estoy mareado.

YOU MIGHT HEAR...

The boat leaves from...
El barco sale de...

The trip/crossing lasts...
El viaje / La travesía dura...

There are ... crossings a day.
Hay ... travesías al día.

The ferry is delayed/cancelled.
El ferry está retrasado / se ha cancelado.

Sea conditions are good/bad.
Las condiciones en el mar son buenas / malas.

VOCABULARY

ferry crossing
la travesía de ferry

ferry terminal
la terminal de ferry

car deck
la cubierta para vehículos

deck
la cubierta

funnel
la chimenea

porthole
el ojo de buey

lifeboat
el bote salvavidas

bow
la proa

stern
la popa

cabin
el camarote

pier
el embarcadero

marina
el puerto deportivo

coastguard
el guardacostas

captain
**el capitán /
la capitana**

crew
la tripulación

foot passenger
**el pasajero de a pie /
la pasajera de a pie**

to board
embarcar(se)

to sail
navegar

to dock
atracar

GENERAL

anchor
el ancla *f*

buoy
la boya

gangway
la pasarela

harbour
el puerto

jetty
el malecón

lifebuoy
el salvavidas

43

lifejacket
el chaleco salvavidas

mooring
el amarradero

port
el puerto

BOATS

canoe
la piragua

ferry
el ferry

inflatable dinghy
el bote inflable

kayak
el kayak

liner
el transatlántico

rowing boat
la barca de remos

sailing boat
el velero

trawler
el pesquero de arrastre

yacht
el yate

IN THE HOME | MI CASA

Spain attracts huge numbers of tourists and expats looking for a place to call "mi casa" for a time, whether it's for a holiday or a longer-term stay. This could be a central city apartment, a cosy "casa rural" in the countryside, or an expansive luxury chalet or villa.

block of flats
el bloque de pisos

roof
el tejado

balcony
el balcón

window
la ventana

THE BASICS | LO ESENCIAL

In Spain, most of the population live in flats in urban areas, although it's quite common for people to head out of the city for "un fin de semana en el campo" (a weekend in the country). Some people will have family homes in their ancestral villages and spend weekends or holidays there.

YOU MIGHT SAY...

I live in...
Vivo en...

I'm staying at...
Me alojo en...

My address is...
Mi dirección es...

I have a flat/house.
Tengo un piso / una casa.

I'm the homeowner/tenant.
Soy el propietario / el inquilino.

I've recently moved.
Me he mudado de casa hace poco.

I'm moving to...
Voy a mudarme de casa a...

I'd like to buy/rent a property here.
Me gustaría comprar / alquilar una casa aquí.

YOU MIGHT HEAR...

Where do you live?
¿Dónde vives?

Where are you staying?
¿Dónde te alojas?

How long have you lived here?
¿Cuánto tiempo llevas viviendo aquí?

What's your address, please?
¿Cuál es tu dirección, por favor?

Are you the owner/tenant?
¿Eres el propietario / el inquilino?

Do you like this area?
¿Te gusta esta zona?

Where are you moving to?
¿A dónde te mudas?

YOU SHOULD KNOW...

You can find properties to rent in Spain that are either furnished ("amueblada") or unfurnished ("sin amueblar"). The rights of tenants are protected by law: make sure you understand what they are if you intend to rent long term in Spain.

VOCABULARY

building
el edificio

apartment
el apartamento

flat
el piso

address
la dirección

suburb
la zona residencial

district
el distrito

letting agent
el agente de alquiler

estate agent
la inmobiliaria

concierge
el portero / la portera

owner
el casero / la casera

neighbour
el vecino / la vecina

tenant
el inquilino / la inquilina

mortgage
la hipoteca

rent
el alquiler

rental agreement
el contrato de alquiler

community charges
los gastos de comunidad

holiday let
el alquiler vacacional

to rent
alquilar

to own
ser dueño / dueña de

to live
vivir

to move house
mudarse de casa

to build a house
construir una casa

TYPES OF BUILDING

apartment block
el bloque de apartamentos

detached house
la casa individual

farmhouse
la casa de labranza

semi-detached house
la casa pareada

studio flat
el estudio

villa
el chalet

THE HOUSE | LA CASA

If you own or rent a house for a longer period of time in Spain, you may need to do some maintenance or even some renovation work on your property.

YOU MIGHT SAY...

We are renovating our home.
Estamos haciendo una reforma en la casa.

We are redecorating the lounge.
Estamos redecorando el salón.

There's a problem with...
Hay un problema con...

It's not working.
No funciona.

The drains are blocked.
Las tuberías están bloqueadas.

The boiler has broken.
Se ha roto la caldera.

There's no hot water.
No hay agua caliente.

We have a power cut.
Se nos ha cortado la electricidad.

I need a plumber/an electrician.
Necesito un fontanero / un electricista.

Can you recommend anyone?
¿Puedes recomendar a alguien?

Can it be repaired?
¿Puede arreglarse?

I can smell gas/smoke.
Huelo a gas / a humo

YOU MIGHT HEAR...

What seems to be the problem?
¿Cuál es el problema?

How long has it been broken/leaking?
¿Cuánto tiempo lleva roto / perdiendo agua?

Where is the meter/fusebox?
¿Dónde está el contador / la caja de fusibles?

Here's a number for a plumber.
Aquí tienes el número de un fontanero.

VOCABULARY

room	attic	(external) wall
la habitación	**el desván**	**el muro**
cellar	ceiling	(internal) wall
el sótano	**el techo**	**la pared**

floor	**el suelo**
plug	**el enchufe**
adaptor	**el adaptador**
socket	**la toma de corriente**
electricity	**la electricidad**
plumbing	**las cañerías**
water pipe	**la tubería del agua**
central heating	**la calefacción central**
satellite dish	**la antena parabólica**
porch	**el porche**
back door	**la puerta trasera**
French windows	**la puertaventana**
roof terrace	**la azotea**
balcony	**el balcón**
skylight	**la claraboya**
to fix	**reparar**
to decorate	**decorar**
to renovate	**reformar**

YOU SHOULD KNOW…

Tradespeople in Spain must be insured and registered.

INSIDE

air conditioning
el aire acondicionado

boiler
la caldera

ceiling fan
el ventilador de techo

extension cable
el alargador

fusebox
la caja de fusibles

light bulb
la bombilla

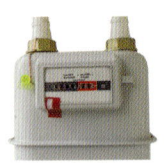

meter
el contador

radiator
el radiador

security alarm
la alarma de seguridad

smoke alarm
la alarma contra incendios

thermostat
el termostato

wood-burning stove
la estufa de leña

OUTSIDE

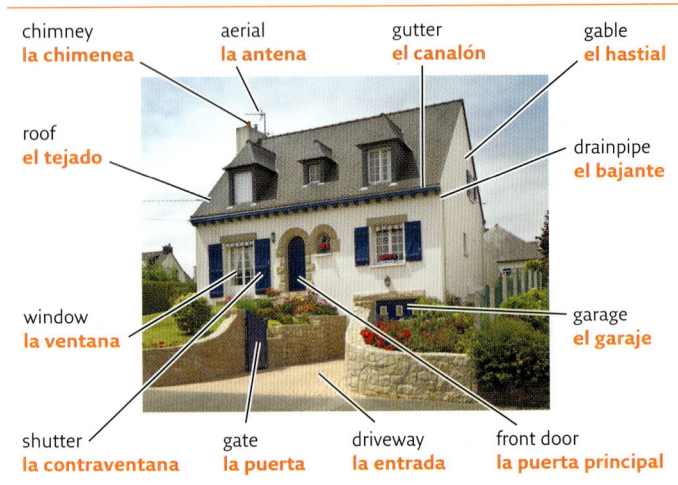

chimney
la chimenea

aerial
la antena

gutter
el canalón

gable
el hastial

roof
el tejado

drainpipe
el bajante

window
la ventana

garage
el garaje

shutter
la contraventana

gate
la puerta

driveway
la entrada

front door
la puerta principal

THE ENTRANCE | LA ENTRADA

YOU MIGHT SAY/HEAR...

Would you like to come round?
¿Te gustaría venir a casa?

Hi! Come in, please.
¡Hola! Entra por favor.

Make yourself at home.
Ponte cómodo.

Shall I take my shoes off?
¿Me quito los zapatos?

Can I use your bathroom?
¿Puedo usar el baño?

Thanks for inviting me over.
Gracias por invitarme.

VOCABULARY

security door
la puerta blindada

corridor
el pasillo

hallway
el vestíbulo de entrada

landing
el distribuidor

stairwell
el hueco de la escalera

lift
el ascensor

peephole
la mirilla

doormat
el felpudo

key
la llave

to buzz somebody in
abrir a alguien por el interfono

to wipe one's feet
limpiarse los pies

to hang one's jacket up
colgar la chaqueta

doorbell
el timbre

intercom
el interfono

letterbox
el buzón

THE LOUNGE | EL SALÓN

VOCABULARY

carpet
la alfombra

floorboard
la tabla del suelo

suite
el tresillo

sofa bed
el sofá cama

table lamp
la lámpara de mesa

home entertainment system
el sistema de entretenimiento en casa

cable/satellite TV
la televisión por cable / satélite

smart TV
la televisión inteligente

TV on demand
la televisión bajo demanda

to relax
relajarse

to sit down
sentarse

to watch TV
ver la tele

GENERAL

bookcase
la librería

curtains
las cortinas

display cabinet
la vitrina

DVD/Blu-ray® player
el reproductor de DVD / Blu-ray®

radio
la radio

remote control
el mando a distancia

sideboard
el aparador

TV stand
la mesa de la tele

Venetian blind
la persiana

LOUNGE

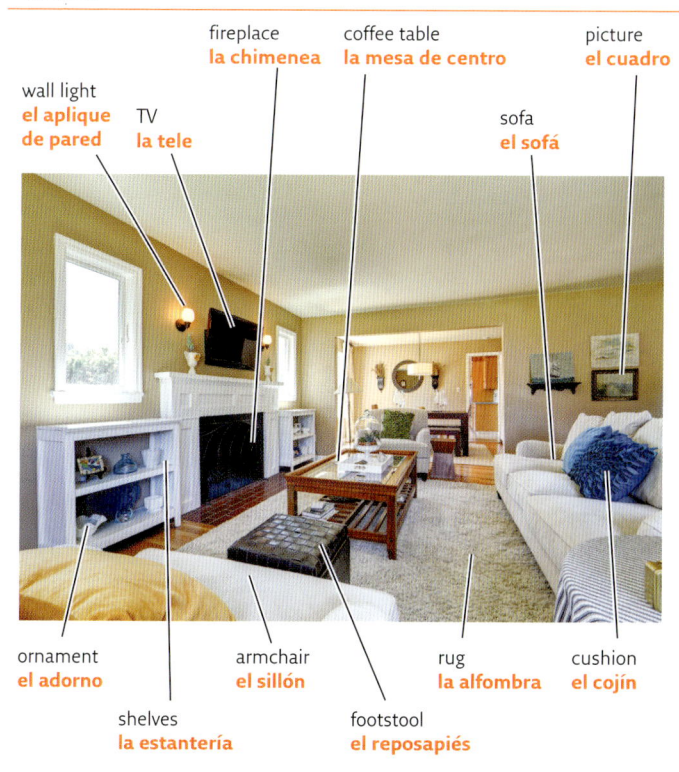

fireplace
la chimenea

coffee table
la mesa de centro

picture
el cuadro

wall light
el aplique de pared

TV
la tele

sofa
el sofá

ornament
el adorno

shelves
la estantería

armchair
el sillón

footstool
el reposapiés

rug
la alfombra

cushion
el cojín

53

THE KITCHEN | LA COCINA

Kitchens in Spain are often closed to the rest of the house and aren't usually treated as entertaining spaces. Open-plan kitchens are known in Spain as "cocinas comedores" (kitchen-dining rooms).

VOCABULARY

(electric) cooker
la cocina

gas cooker
la cocina de gas

toaster
el tostador

kettle
el hervidor de agua

to cook/bake
cocinar

to fry
freír

to stir-fry
sofreír

to boil
hervir

to roast
asar

to wash up
lavar (los platos)

to clean the worktops
limpiar la encimera

to put away the groceries
guardar la compra

MISCELLANEOUS ITEMS

aluminium foil
el papel de aluminio

bread bin
la panera

clingfilm
el film transparente

fruit bowl
la frutera

kitchen roll
el papel de cocina

pedal bin
el cubo de pedal

KITCHEN UTENSILS

baking tray
la bandeja del horno

casserole dish
la cazuela

chopping board
la tabla de cortar

coffee pot
la cafetera

colander
el escurridor

corkscrew
el sacacorchos

deep-fat fryer
la freidora

food processor
el robot de cocina

frying pan
la sartén

grater
el rallador

hand blender
la batidora de mano

hand mixer
la batidora manual

kitchen knife
el cuchillo de cocina

ladle
el cucharón

measuring jug
la jarra medidora

mixing bowl
el recipiente para mezclar

paella pan
la paellera

peeler
el pelador

pressure cooker
la olla exprés

rolling pin
el rodillo de cocina

saucepan
el cazo

sieve
el tamiz

spatula
la espátula

tin opener
el abrelatas

whisk
la batidora

wok
el wok

wooden spoon
la cuchara de madera

THE KITCHEN

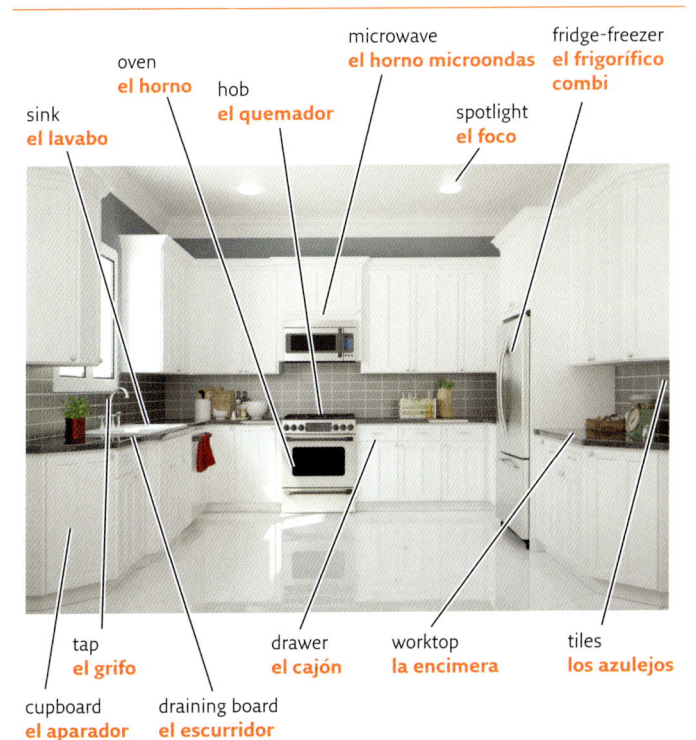

sink
el lavabo

oven
el horno

hob
el quemador

microwave
el horno microondas

fridge-freezer
el frigorífico combi

spotlight
el foco

tap
el grifo

cupboard
el aparador

draining board
el escurridor

drawer
el cajón

worktop
la encimera

tiles
los azulejos

THE DINING ROOM | EL COMEDOR

VOCABULARY

dining table **la mesa de comedor**	crockery **la vajilla**	to set the table **poner la mesa**
place mat **el mantelito individual**	cutlery **los cubiertos**	to dine **cenar**
coaster **el posavasos**	glassware **la cristalería**	to clear the table **recoger la mesa**

YOU SHOULD KNOW...

In Spanish homes, it is good table manners to keep your hands on the table and to say "que aproveche" (enjoy your meal) to your fellow diners before you begin your meal.

GENERAL

gravy boat
la salsera

napkin
la servilleta

pepper mill
el molinillo de pimienta

salad bowl
la ensaladera

salt cellar
el molinillo de sal

serving dish
la fuente de servir

TABLE SETTINGS

bowl
el cuenco

champagne flute
la copa de cava

cup and saucer
la taza y el platillo

plate
el plato

knife and fork
el cuchillo y el tenedor

spoon
la cuchara

teaspoon
la cucharilla

tumbler
el vaso

wine glass
la copa de vino

THE BEDROOM | EL DORMITORIO

VOCABULARY

single bed
la cama individual

double bed
la cama de matrimonio

truckle bed
la cama nido

bunk beds
las literas

bedding
la ropa de cama

master bedroom
el dormitorio principal

spare bedroom
el cuarto de invitados

en-suite bathroom
el baño integrado

nursery
la habitación del bebé

to go to bed
irse a la cama

to sleep
dormir

to wake up
despertarse

to make the bed
hacer la cama

to change the sheets
cambiar las sábanas

GENERAL

blanket
la manta

clock radio
la radio despertador

coat hanger
la percha

dressing table
el tocador

hairdryer
el secador de pelo

laundry basket
la cesta de la ropa sucia

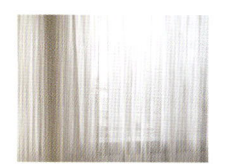

net curtains
los visillos

quilt
el edredón

sheets
las sábanas

BEDROOM

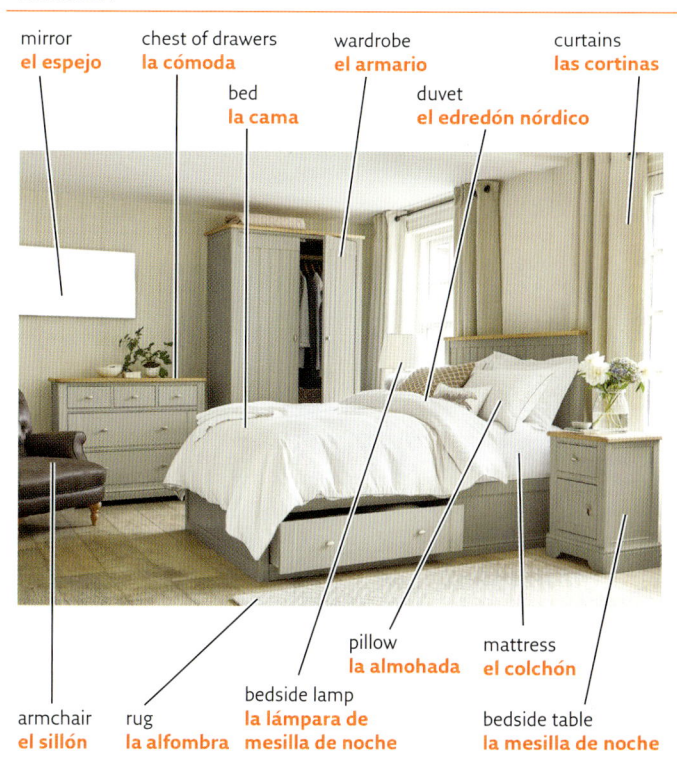

mirror
el espejo

chest of drawers
la cómoda

wardrobe
el armario

curtains
las cortinas

bed
la cama

duvet
el edredón nórdico

pillow
la almohada

mattress
el colchón

armchair
el sillón

rug
la alfombra

bedside lamp
la lámpara de mesilla de noche

bedside table
la mesilla de noche

THE BATHROOM | EL BAÑO

Many people in Spain live in flats, and so often don't have space for a bathtub in their bathrooms.

VOCABULARY

shower curtain
la cortina de baño

toilet seat
el asiento de retrete

flush
la cisterna

drain
el sumidero

to shower
ducharse

to have a bath
bañarse

to wash one's hands
lavarse las manos

to brush one's teeth
cepillarse los dientes

to go to the toilet
ir al servicio

GENERAL

bath mat
la alfombrilla de baño

bath towel
la toalla de baño

hand towel
la toalla de mano

shower puff
la esponja de malla

soap
el jabón

soap dish
la jabonera

sponge
la esponja

toilet brush
la escobilla del váter

toilet roll
el rollo de papel higiénico

BATHROOM

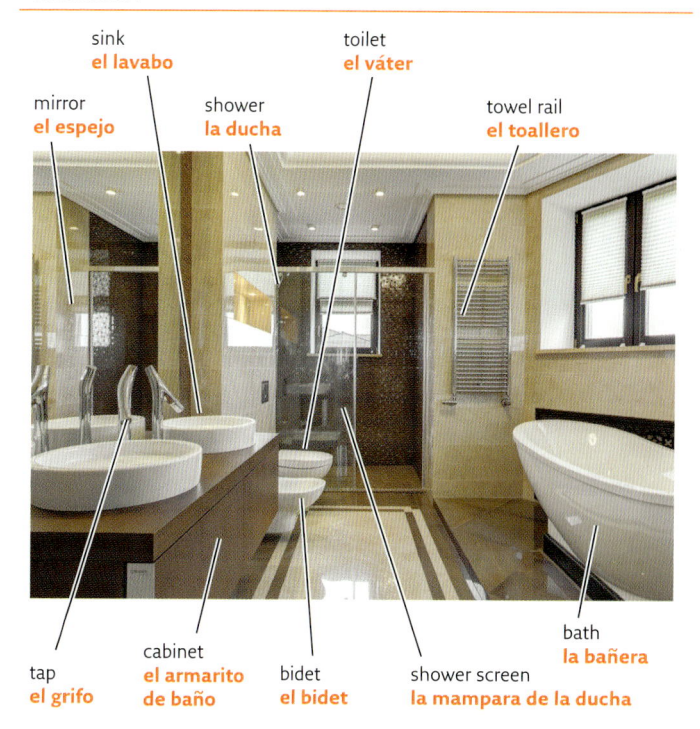

sink
el lavabo

toilet
el váter

mirror
el espejo

shower
la ducha

towel rail
el toallero

tap
el grifo

cabinet
el armarito de baño

bidet
el bidet

shower screen
la mampara de la ducha

bath
la bañera

63

THE GARDEN | EL JARDÍN

VOCABULARY

tree
el árbol

soil
la tierra

grass
el césped

plant
la planta

weed
la mala hierba

flowerbed
el parterre

compost
el abono

allotment
el huerto urbano

greenhouse
el invernadero

gardener
**el jardinero /
la jardinera**

to weed
quitar la maleza

to water
regar

to grow
cultivar

to plant
plantar

GENERAL

awning
el toldo

decking
la tarima

garden fork
la horquilla de jardín

garden hose
la manguera

gardening gloves
los guantes de jardinería

garden shed
el cobertizo

hoe **el azadón**	lawnmower **el cortacésped**	parasol **el parasol**
plant pot **la maceta**	pruners **las tijeras de poda**	spade **la pala**
trowel **la paleta**	watering can **la regadera**	weedkiller **el herbicida**
Wellington boots **las botas de goma**	wheelbarrow **la carretilla**	windowbox **la jardinera**

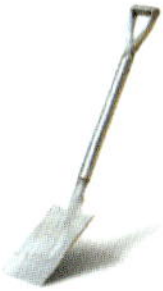

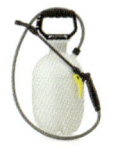

GARDEN

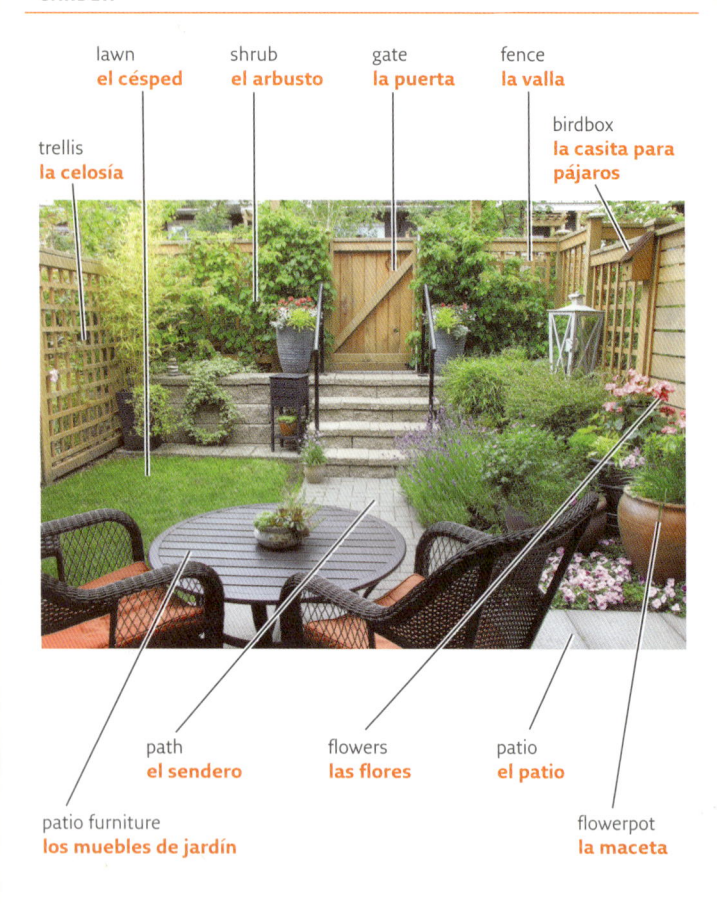

lawn
el césped

shrub
el arbusto

gate
la puerta

fence
la valla

trellis
la celosía

birdbox
la casita para pájaros

path
el sendero

flowers
las flores

patio
el patio

patio furniture
los muebles de jardín

flowerpot
la maceta

66

HOUSEWORK | LAS LABORES DE LA CASA

VOCABULARY

utility room
el lavadero

household appliances
los electrodomésticos

chores
las tareas de la casa

wastepaper basket
la papelera

basin
la palangana

bleach
la lejía

disinfectant
el desinfectante

dishwasher tablet
la pastilla del lavavajillas

laundry detergent
el detergente de ropa

washing-up liquid
el lavavajillas

bin bag
la bolsa de la basura

to sweep the floor
barrer el suelo

to do the laundry
hacer la colada

to hoover
pasar la aspiradora

to tidy up
recoger

to clean
limpiar

to take out the bin
sacar la basura

to iron
planchar

to dust
quitar el polvo

brush
la escoba

bucket
el cubo

cloth
el trapo

clothes horse
el tendedero

clothes pegs
las pinzas de la ropa

dishwasher
el lavavajillas

67

dustbin
el cubo de la basura

dustpan
el recogedor

iron
la plancha

ironing board
la tabla de planchar

mop
la fregona

rubber gloves
los guantes de goma

scourer
el estropajo

tea towel
el paño de cocina

tumble drier
la secadora

vacuum cleaner
la aspiradora

washing line
la cuerda para tender

washing machine
la lavadora

AT THE SHOPS | EN LAS TIENDAS

Wonderful displays of cured meats and shellfish in lively food markets, fashionable clothes and shoes in popular Spanish high street shops – just some of the things that might spring to mind when it comes to shopping in Spain. That's not to say that you won't find plenty of large supermarkets, busy shopping centres, and many familiar international chains in urban areas.

basket
la cesta

banana
el plátano

bread
el pan

vegetable oil
el aceite vegetal

THE BASICS | LO ESENCIAL

Most stores in Spain are open from Monday to Saturday from around 9.30 a.m. till 8 p.m. and shut between 1.30 and 5 p.m. for lunch. Bigger shops have extended hours and often open on Sundays. Shops in tourist destinations and certain convenience stores are able to stay open till late, sometimes well into the night.

YOU MIGHT SAY...

Where is the...?
¿Dónde está el / la...?

Where is the nearest...?
¿Dónde está el ... más cercano / la ... más cercana?

Where can I buy...?
¿Dónde puedo comprar...?

What time do you open/close?
¿A qué hora abren / cierran?

I'm just looking, thanks.
Solo estoy mirando, gracias.

Do you sell...?
¿Venden...?

May I have...?
¿Me pondría...?

Can I pay by cash/card?
¿Puedo pagar en efectivo / con tarjeta?

Can I pay with my mobile app?
¿Puedo pagar con la aplicación de mi teléfono?

How much does this cost?
¿Cuánto cuesta?

How much is delivery?
¿Cuánto cuesta la entrega?

I need...
Necesito...

I would like...
Quería...

Can I exchange this?
¿Puedo cambiar esto?

Can I get a refund?
¿Podrían reembolsarme el dinero?

That's all, thank you.
Eso es todo, gracias.

YOU SHOULD KNOW...

Distribution of single-use plastic bags is banned in Spanish shops, but reusable plastic bags and paper bags can be purchased in most stores.

YOU MIGHT HEAR...

Are you being served?
¿Le atienden?

Would you like anything else?
¿Quiere algo más?

It costs...
Cuesta...

I'm sorry, we don't have...
Lo siento, no tenemos...

I can order that for you.
Puedo encargárselo.

How would you like to pay?
¿Cómo desea pagar?

Can you enter your PIN?
¿Puede introducir su PIN?

Would you like a receipt?
¿Quiere el tique de compra?

Would you like a gift receipt?
¿Quiere tique regalo?

We don't offer refunds/exchanges.
No reembolsamos / cambiamos el producto.

Have you got a receipt?
¿Tiene el tique de compra?

Have a good day!
Que tenga un buen día.

VOCABULARY

shop
la tienda

shopping centre
el centro comercial

supermarket
el supermercado

market
el mercado

retail chain
la cadena comercial

cash
el dinero en efectivo

change
la vuelta

contactless
sin contacto

gift voucher
el cheque regalo

PIN
el PIN

exchange
el cambio

refund
el reintegro

voucher
el vale

shop assistant
el dependiente / la dependienta

to browse
mirar

to buy
comprar

to pay
pagar

to shop (online)
comprar (en línea)

to do the shopping
hacer la compra

banknotes
los billetes de banco

card reader
el lector de tarjetas

coins
las monedas

debit/credit card
la tarjeta de débito / crédito

paper bag
la bolsa de papel

plastic bag
la bolsa de plástico

reusable shopping bag
la bolsa reutilizable

receipt
el tique de compra

till point
la caja

SUPERMARKET | EL SUPERMERCADO

Shopping for groceries over the internet is less prevalent in Spain than in the UK, but it is a growing trend. Online shopping or delivery services are offered by most major Spanish supermarkets, but availability will vary from region to region. Bear in mind that it is rare to find 24-hour shops and supermarkets, even in the biggest cities in Spain.

YOU MIGHT SAY...

Where can I find...?
¿Dónde puedo encontrar...?

I'm looking for...
Busco...

Do you have...?
¿Tiene...?

Do you have carrier bags?
¿Tiene bolsas?

Can you give me a plastic bag?
¿Me da una bolsa de plástico?

YOU MIGHT HEAR...

We have/don't have...
Tenemos / No tenemos...

It's in aisle 1/2/3.
Está en el pasillo número 1 / 2 / 3.

Can I help you with your bags?
¿Puedo ayudarle con las bolsas?

There is a charge for a carrier bag.
Se cobra por las bolsas.

Do you have a loyalty card?
¿Tiene tarjeta de puntos?

VOCABULARY

groceries
los comestibles

aisle
el pasillo

loyalty card
la tarjeta de puntos

delicatessen
la tienda de delicatessen

ready meal
la comida preparada

bottle
la botella

box
la caja

carton
el cartón

jar
el tarro

packet
el paquete

tin
la lata

tinned
enlatado

fresh
fresco

frozen
congelado

GENERAL

basket
la cesta

scales
el peso

trolley
el carro

GROCERIES

biscuits
las galletas

couscous
el cous cous

herbs
las hierbas

honey
la miel

icing sugar
el azúcar glas

instant coffee
el café instantáneo

jam
la mermelada

ketchup
el ketchup

lentils
las lentejas

marmalade
la mermelada de naranja

mayonnaise
la mayonesa

olive oil
el aceite de oliva

pasta
la pasta

pepper
la pimienta

rice
el arroz

salt
la sal

spices
las especias

sugar
el azúcar

teabags
las bolsitas de té

vegetable oil
el aceite vegetal

vinegar
el vinagre

SNACKS

chocolate
el chocolate

crisps
las patatas fritas

nuts
los frutos secos

olives
las aceitunas

popcorn
las palomitas

sweets
las golosinas

DRINKS

beer
la cerveza

fizzy drink
la bebida con burbujas

fruit juice
el zumo de frutas

spirits
las bebidas alcohólicas

still/sparkling water
el agua sin gas / con gas

wine
el vino

MARKET | EL MERCADO

Local markets will be found in most Spanish villages, towns, and cities, with farmers' markets ("mercados de productores") growing increasingly popular. Many also double as bustling tapas and street food establishments.

YOU MIGHT SAY...

Where is the market?
¿Dónde está el mercado?

When is market day?
¿Qué día hay mercado?

Who's next?
¿Quién da la vez?

A kilo of...
Un kilo de...

100 grams of...
100 gramos de...

What do I owe you?
¿Cuánto le debo?

YOU MIGHT HEAR...

The market is in the square.
El mercado es en la plaza.

The market is on a Tuesday.
Hay mercado los martes.

I'm next.
Yo doy la vez.

What can I get you?
¿Qué le pongo?

Here you go. Anything else?
Aquí tiene. ¿Algo más?

Here's your change.
Aquí tiene el cambio.

VOCABULARY

marketplace
la plaza

flea market
el mercadillo

indoor market
el mercado cubierto

farmers' market
el mercado de productores

local
local

organic
ecológico

seasonal
de temporada

home-made
casero

YOU SHOULD KNOW...

Haggling would not be expected at the stalls of a fruit and vegetable market; it's a different story at the flea market!

MARKETPLACE

customers
los clientes

stall
el puesto

trader
**el comerciante /
la comerciante**

basket
la cesta

plastic bag
la bolsa de plástico

produce
los productos

crate
la caja

FRUIT AND VEGETABLES | LAS FRUTAS Y VERDURAS

YOU MIGHT SAY...

Do you have...?
¿Tiene...?

Are they ripe/fresh?
¿Están maduros / frescos?

YOU MIGHT HEAR...

What would you like?
¿Qué desea?

They are very fresh.
Son muy frescos.

VOCABULARY

grocer's **la tienda de comestibles**	seed **la semilla**	unripe **verde**
juice **el zumo**	segment **el gajo**	seedless **sin semillas**
leaf **la hoja**	skin **la piel**	to chop **cortar**
peel **la piel**	stone **el hueso**	to dice **cortar en cuadritos**
pip **la pepita**	fresh **fresco**	to grate **rallar**
rind **la cáscara**	rotten **podrido**	to juice **hacer zumo**
	ripe **maduro**	to peel **pelar**

YOU SHOULD KNOW...

When buying fruit or vegetables from the supermarket, customers are usually required to weigh and sticker their purchases before going to the checkouts.

FRUIT

apple
la manzana

apricot
el albaricoque

banana
el plátano

blackberry
la mora

blueberry
el arándano

cherry
la cereza

grape
la uva

grapefruit
el pomelo

kiwi fruit
el kiwi

lemon
el limón

mango
el mango

melon
el melón

orange
la naranja

papaya
la papaya

passion fruit
el maracuyá

peach
el melocotón

pear
la pera

pineapple
la piña

plum
la ciruela

pomegranate
la granada

raspberry
la frambuesa

redcurrant
la grosella roja

strawberry
la fresa

watermelon
la sandía

VEGETABLES

artichoke
la alcachofa

asparagus
el espárrago

aubergine
la berenjena

beetroot
la remolacha

broccoli
el brócoli

Brussels sprout
la col de Bruselas

cabbage
la col

carrot
la zanahoria

cauliflower
la coliflor

celery
el apio

chilli
el chile

courgette
el calabacín

cucumber
el pepino

garlic
el ajo

green beans
las judías verdes

leek
el puerro

lettuce
la lechuga

mushroom
el champiñón

onion
la cebolla

peas
el guisante

potato
la patata

red pepper
el pimiento rojo

spinach
la espinaca

tomato
el tomate

BAKERY AND PATISSERIE | LA PANADERÍA-PASTELERÍA

A trip to the bakery to buy the daily "barra de pan" (literally "bar of bread") is part of daily life in Spain. Many bakeries will also offer other traditional varieties of bread, some made with corn, or even potato.

YOU MIGHT SAY...

Do you sell...?
¿Venden...?

Could I have...?
¿Me pone...?

How much are...?
¿Cuánto cuestan...?

YOU MIGHT HEAR...

Are you being served?
¿Le atienden?

Would you like anything else?
¿Quiere algo más?

It costs...
Cuesta...

VOCABULARY

baker
el panadero / la panadera

bread
el pan

wholemeal bread
el pan integral

slice
la rodaja

crust
la corteza

dough
la masa

flour
la harina

gluten-free
sin gluten

to bake
cocinar

YOU SHOULD KNOW...

You can buy most sweet pastries in a "panadería" (bakery) but, for more elaborate cakes, head to a "pastelería" (patisserie).

baguette
la barra de pan

bread rolls
los panecillos

churros
los churros

croissant
el croissant

Danish pastry
el pastel de hojaldre

doughnut
el donut

éclair
el petisú

fruit tart
la tartaleta de fruta

mille-feuille
la milhoja

muffin
la magdalena

pancakes
las tortitas

pasty
la empanada

round loaf
la hogaza de pan

sliced bread
el pan de molde

waffle
el gofre

BUTCHER'S | LA CARNICERÍA

Butchers in Spain are often able to recommend what kind of cuts to buy for the recipes you'd like to try, as well as local specialities they may sell.

YOU MIGHT SAY...

A slice of ..., please.
Una rodaja de ..., por favor.

Can you slice this for me, please?
¿Puede cortármelo en rodajas, por favor?

Could you prepare it for a roast, please?
¿Podría preparármelo para asado?

YOU MIGHT HEAR...

Certainly, sir/madam.
Por supuesto, señor / señora.

How much would you like?
¿Cuánto quiere?

How many would you like?
¿Cuántos quiere?

VOCABULARY

butcher
el carnicero / la carnicera

meat
la carne

white meat
la carne blanca

red meat
la carne roja

cold meats
el fiambre

pâté
el paté

beef
la carne de vaca

lamb
el cordero

pork
la carne de cerdo

poultry
las aves de corral

duck
el pato

goose
la oca

rabbit
el conejo

game
la caza

veal
la ternera

venison
el venado

offal
las asaduras

free-range
de granja

organic
ecológico

raw
crudo

cooked
cocido

bacon **el beicon**	burger **la hamburguesa**	chicken breast **la pechuga de pollo**
chop **la chuleta**	chorizo **el chorizo**	fillet **el filete**
ham **el jamón**	joint **la pieza de carne para asar**	mince **la carne picada**
ribs **el costillar**	sausage **la salchicha**	steak **el bistec**

FISHMONGER'S | LA PESCADERÍA

Spanish people eat a great deal of fish and shellfish – there are many excellent fishmongers where you can ask for tips on what is fresh, what has been frozen, and what is in season.

YOU MIGHT SAY...

How fresh is this fish?
¿Es fresco este pescado?

I'd like this filleted/in steaks, please.
¿Me lo hace en filetes / rodajas, por favor?

Can you remove the bones?
¿Puede quitarle las espinas?

Is it sustainably caught fish?
¿Es pescado sostenible?

YOU MIGHT HEAR...

It was landed...
Lo pescaron...

This fish is frozen.
El pescado es congelado.

Would you like this filleted?
¿Quiere que se lo haga en filetes?

Yes, I can do that for you.
Sí, ahora se lo hago.

VOCABULARY

(fish)bone
la espina (de pescado)

deboned
sin espinas

fishmonger
el pescadero / la pescadera

fillet
el filete

filleted
en filetes

scales
las escamas

shellfish
el marisco

shell
la concha

freshwater
de agua dulce

saltwater
de agua salada

farmed
de piscifactoría

wild
salvaje

salted
salado

smoked
ahumado

FISH

cod
el bacalao

hake
la merluza

herring
el arenque

mackerel
la caballa

monkfish
el rape

salmon
el salmón

sardine
la sardina

sea bass
la lubina

sea bream
la dorada

skate
la raya

trout
la trucha

tuna
el atún

SEAFOOD

clam
la almeja

cockle
el berberecho

crab
el cangrejo

crayfish
el cangrejo de río

lobster
la langosta

mussel
el mejillón

octopus
el pulpo

oyster
la ostra

prawn
la gamba

scallop
la vieira

shrimp
el camarón

squid
el calamar

CHEESE AND DAIRY PRODUCTS | EL QUESO Y LOS LÁCTEOS

UHT milk is much more widely used in Spain than in the UK, but it is possible to find fresh milk ("leche fresca") in the supermarkets.

VOCABULARY

egg white
la clara de huevo

egg yolk
la yema de huevo

soymilk
la leche de soja

UHT milk
la leche UHT

whole milk
la leche entera

skimmed/
semi-skimmed milk
la leche desnatada / semidesnatada

single/double cream
la nata líquida / para montar

free-range
de granja

pasteurized/
unpasteurized
pasteurizado / no pasteurizado

blue cheese
el queso azul

cheese
el queso

cream cheese
el queso crema

GENERAL

butter
la mantequilla

cream
la nata

egg
el huevo

margarine
la margarina

milk
la leche

yoghurt
el yogurt

CHEESE

brie
el brie

Cabrales
el cabrales

cheddar
el queso cheddar

Emmenthal
el emmental

goat's cheese
el queso de cabra

Mahon cheese
el queso de Mahón

Manchego
el manchego

mozzarella
la mozzarella

parmesan
el parmesano

ricotta
el requesón

sheep's milk cheese
el queso de oveja

smoked cheese
el queso ahumado

PHARMACY | LA FARMACIA

In Spain, pharmacies are owned and run by individual pharmacists, meaning you don't see pharmacy chains in Spanish towns and villages. You can also have your blood pressure checked or get advice on how to treat minor ailments.

YOU MIGHT SAY...

I need something for...
Necesito algo para...

I'm allergic to...
Soy alérgico a...

I'm collecting a prescription.
Vengo a recoger una receta.

What do you recommend?
¿Qué recomienda?

Is it suitable for young children?
¿Lo pueden tomar los niños?

YOU MIGHT HEAR...

Do you have a prescription?
¿Tiene la receta?

Do you have your health card?
¿Tiene la tarjeta sanitaria?

Do you have any allergies?
¿Tiene alguna alergia?

Take two tablets twice a day.
Tome dos pastillas dos veces al día.

You should see a doctor.
Debería ir al médico.

I'd recommend...
Le recomiendo...

VOCABULARY

pharmacist
el farmacéutico / la farmacéutica

prescription
la receta

cold
el resfriado

diarrhoea
la diarrea

hay fever
la alergia al polen

headache
el dolor de cabeza

sore throat
el dolor de garganta

stomachache
el dolor de estómago

antihistamine
el antihistamínico

decongestant
el descongestivo

painkiller
el calmante

handwash
el jabón líquido para las manos

GENERAL

antiseptic
el antiséptico

bandage
el vendaje

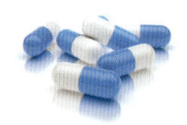

capsule
la cápsula

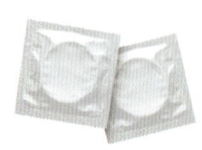

condom
el preservativo

cough mixture
el jarabe para la tos

drops
las gotas

insect repellent
el repelente de insectos

lozenges
las pastillas para la garganta

medicine
la medicina

plaster
la tirita

suntan lotion
la loción bronceadora

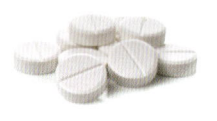

tablet/pill
la pastilla

HYGIENE

antiperspirant
el desodorante

conditioner
el suavizante

mouthwash
el enjuague bucal

razor
la cuchilla de afeitar

sanitary towel
la compresa

shampoo
el champú

shaving foam
la espuma de afeitar

shower gel
el gel de ducha

soap
el jabón

tampon
el tampón

toothbrush
el cepillo de dientes

toothpaste
el dentífrico

BEAUTY

blusher
el colorete

comb
el peine

eyeliner
el delineador

eyeshadow
la sombra de ojos

foundation
la base

hairbrush
el cepillo

hairspray
la laca para el pelo

lip balm
el bálsamo de labios

lipstick
el pintalabios

mascara
el rímel

nail varnish
el esmalte de uñas

(face) powder
el polvo facial

BABY GOODS | PARA BEBÉ

If you intend to travel to Spain with your baby, it may be possible to hire the equipment you require from specialist companies.

VOCABULARY

colic
los cólicos

nappy rash
la escocedura

disposable nappy
el pañal desechable

reusable nappy
el pañal reutilizable

nappy sack
la bolsa para pañales

teething gel
el gel para los primeros dientes

to breast-feed
dar el pecho

to be teething
estar echando los dientes

CLOTHING

babygro®/sleepsuit
el pelele

bib
el babero

bootees
las botitas

mittens
las manoplas

snowsuit
el mono

vest
el body

97

HEALTH AND HYGIENE

baby food
la comida para bebé

baby lotion
la loción para bebé

baby's bottle
el biberón

changing bag
el bolso cambiador

cotton bud
el bastoncillo

cotton wool
el algodón

formula milk
la fórmula

nappy
el pañal

nappy cream
la crema de pañal

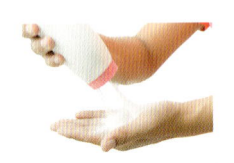

talcum powder
los polvos de talco

teething ring
el anillo de dentición

wet wipes
las toallitas húmedas

ACCESSORIES

baby bath
la bañera para bebé

baby seat
la sillita de coche para niño

baby sling
el portabebés

baby walker
el andador

cot
la cuna

dummy
el chupete

highchair
la trona

mobile
el móvil

Moses basket
el moisés

pram
el cochecito

pushchair
la sillita

travel cot
la cuna de viaje

TOBACCONIST | EL ESTANCO

Tobacco, stamps, postcards, envelopes, and stationery items are all available at "el estanco". They can also sell newspapers, magazines, and confectionery, and it's also possible to buy top-ups for public transport travel cards at many stores.

VOCABULARY

kiosk **el quiosco**	tabloid **el tabloide**	daily **diario**
newspaper stand **el puesto de periódicos**	stationery **los artículos de escritorio**	weekly **semanal**
broadsheet **el periódico de gran formato**	vendor **el vendedor / la vendedora**	

GENERAL

cigar **el cigarro**

cigarette **el cigarrillo**

comic book **el cómic**

confectionery **los productos de confitería**

e-cigarette **el cigarrillo electrónico**

envelope **el sobre**

greetings card
la tarjeta de felicitación

magazine
la revista

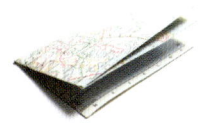

map
el mapa

newspaper
el periódico

notebook
el cuaderno

pen
el bolígrafo

pencil
el lápiz

postcard
la postal

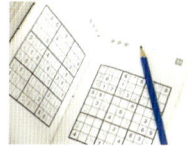

puzzle book
la revista de rompecabezas

scratch card
la tarjeta de rasque y gane

stamp
el sello

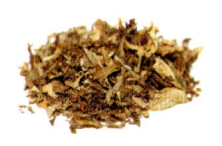

tobacco
el tabaco

101

DEPARTMENT STORE | LOS GRANDES ALMACENES

YOU MIGHT SAY...

Where is the menswear department?
¿Dónde está el departamento de caballeros?

Which floor is this?
¿En qué planta estamos?

Can you gift-wrap this, please?
¿Me lo puede envolver para regalo, por favor?

Where are the escalators/lifts?
¿Dónde están las escaleras mecánicas / los ascensores?

YOU MIGHT HEAR...

Menswear is on the second floor.
El departamento de caballeros está en la segunda planta.

This is the first floor.
Esta es la primera planta.

Would you like this gift-wrapped?
¿Quiere que se lo envuelva para regalo?

The escalators/lifts are...
Las escaleras mecánicas / Los ascensores están...

VOCABULARY

brand
la marca

counter
el mostrador

department
el departamento

menswear
la ropa de hombre

sportswear
la ropa de deporte

swimwear
los trajes de baño

womenswear
la ropa de mujer

escalators
las escaleras mecánicas

floor
la planta

lift
el ascensor

luxury
lujoso

sale
las rebajas

YOU SHOULD KNOW...

Note that while many smaller stores will close at midday for lunch, many department stores will remain open for the whole afternoon – a practice known as "el horario continuo" in Spain.

accessories
los accesorios

cosmetics
los cosméticos

fashion
la moda

food and drink
la comida y la bebida

footwear
el calzado

furniture
el mobiliario

kitchenware
los artículos de cocina

leather goods
los artículos de cuero

lighting
la iluminación

lingerie
la lencería

soft furnishings
las telas para cortinas y tapicerías

toys
los juguetes

CLOTHING AND FOOTWEAR | LA ROPA Y EL CALZADO

Spanish high streets are filled with many popular clothes shops and chains, some of which are recognised all over the world. Spain is also well known for its producers of high-quality shoes and footwear.

YOU MIGHT SAY...

I'm just looking, thanks.
Solo estoy mirando, gracias.

I'd like to try this on, please.
Me gustaría probarme esto, por favor.

Where are the fitting rooms?
¿Dónde están los probadores?

I'm a size...
Tengo la talla...

Have you got a bigger/smaller size? (clothing)
¿Tiene una talla más grande / más pequeña?

Have you got a bigger/smaller size? (shoes)
¿Tiene un número más grande / más pequeño?

This is too small/big.
Es demasiado pequeño / grande.

This is too short/long.
Es demasiado corto / largo.

This is torn.
Está roto.

It's not my style.
No es mi estilo.

YOU MIGHT HEAR...

Can I help you?
¿Puedo ayudarle?

Let me know if I can help.
Llámeme si necesita ayuda.

The fitting rooms are over there.
Los probadores están allí.

What size are you? (clothing)
¿Qué talla usa?

What size are you? (shoes)
¿Qué número calza?

I can get you another size.
Le puedo traer otra talla.

I'm sorry, it's out of stock.
Lo siento, se nos ha agotado.

I'm sorry, we don't have that size/colour.
Lo siento, no nos queda de esa talla / ese color.

That suits you.
Le queda bien.

VOCABULARY

clothes/clothing **la ropa**	umbrella **el paraguas**	silk **la seda**
shoes **los zapatos**	casual **de sport**	wool **la lana**
underwear **la ropa interior**	smart **elegante**	size (clothing) **la talla**
fitting room **el probador**	denim **la tela vaquera**	size (shoe) **el número**
purse **el monedero**	cotton **el algodón**	petite **petite**
wallet **la cartera**	polyester **el poliéster**	plus-size **tallas grandes**
jewellery **las joyas**	leather **la piel**	to try on **probarse**

CLOTHING

bikini
el bikini

blouse
la blusa

boxer shorts
los calzoncillos

bra
el sujetador

cardigan
la chaqueta de punto

coat
el abrigo

105

dress
el vestido

dressing gown
la bata

dungarees
el peto

jacket
la chaqueta

jeans
los vaqueros

jogging bottoms
los pantalones de chándal

jumper
el suéter

leggings
las mallas

pants
las bragas

pyjamas
el pijama

shirt
la camisa

shorts
el pantalón corto

skirt
la falda

socks
los calcetines

sweatshirt
la sudadera

swimsuit
el traje de baño

(three-piece) suit
el traje de tres piezas

tie
la corbata

tights
las medias

trousers
el pantalón

T-shirt
la camiseta

ACCCESSORIES

baseball cap
la gorra de béisbol

belt
el cinturón

bracelet
la pulsera

earrings
los pendientes

gloves
los guantes

handbag
el bolso

necklace
el collar

scarf
la bufanda

woolly hat
el gorro de lana

FOOTWEAR

boots
las botas

high heels
los zapatos de tacón alto

lace-up shoes
los zapatos con cordones

sandals
las sandalias

slippers
las zapatillas

trainers
las deportivas

DIY STORE | LA TIENDA DE BRICOLAJE

VOCABULARY

hardware shop
la ferretería

home improvements
las mejoras del hogar

tool
la herramienta

power tool
la herramienta eléctrica

tool box
la caja de herramientas

to do DIY
hacer bricolaje

chisel
el cincel

electric drill
el taladro eléctrico

hacksaw
la sierra de arco

hammer
el martillo

light bulb
la bombilla

nails
los clavos

nuts and bolts
los tornillos y las tuercas

paint
la pintura

paintbrush
el pincel

paint roller
el rodillo de pintura

pliers
los alicates

saw
la sierra

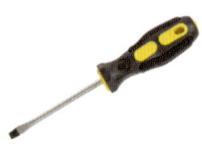

screwdriver
el destornillador

screws
los tornillos tirafondos

spanner
la llave inglesa

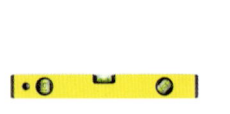

spirit level
el nivel de burbuja

stepladder
la escalera de mano

tilecutter
el cortador de baldosas

tiles
las baldosas

wallpaper
el papel pintado

wrench
la llave inglesa

OTHER SHOPS | OTRAS TIENDAS

antique shop
la tienda de antigüedades

barber's
la peluquería

beauty salon
el salón de belleza

bookshop
la librería

boutique
la boutique

car showroom
el concesionario de automóviles

charity shop
la tienda solidaria de segunda mano

electrical store
la tienda de electrodomésticos

estate agency
la agencia inmobiliaria

florist's
la floristería

furniture store
la tienda de muebles

garden centre
el vivero

gift shop
la tienda de artículos para regalo

hairdresser's
la peluquería

health food shop
el herbolario

jeweller's
la joyería

music shop
la tienda de música

optician's
el oculista

pet shop
la tienda de mascotas

phone shop
la tienda de telefonía móvil

shoe shop
la zapatería

toyshop
la juguetería

travel agency
la agencia de viajes

wine shop
la tienda de vinos

DAY-TO-DAY | EL DÍA A DÍA

Business meetings, meals with friends, or courses of study... whatever your day-to-day schedule looks like during your time in Spain, you will require some basic vocabulary when going on errands, planning outings, and going about your everyday business.

coffee with milk
el café con leche

handle
el asa *f*

cup
la taza

saucer
el platillo

THE BASICS | LO ESENCIAL

Here are a few basic words and phrases for describing your day-to-day routine ("el día a día"), and making plans with others.

YOU MIGHT SAY...

Where are you going?
¿A dónde vas?

What time do you finish?
¿A qué hora terminas?

What are you doing today/tonight?
¿Qué vas a hacer hoy / esta noche?

Are you free on Friday?
¿Estás libre el viernes?

Would you like to meet up?
¿Quieres quedar?

Where/When would you like to meet?
¿Dónde / Cuándo te gustaría quedar?

YOU MIGHT HEAR...

I'm at work/uni.
Estoy en la oficina / en la universidad.

I have a day off.
Tengo el día libre.

I've got an appointment.
Tengo una cita.

I'm going to...
Voy a...

I'll be back by...
Volveré a las...

I'll meet you at...
Quedamos en...

I can't meet up today, sorry.
Hoy no puedo quedar, lo siento.

VOCABULARY

to wake up **despertarse**	to arrive **llegar**	to meet friends **quedar con amigos**
to get dressed **vestirse**	to leave **salir**	to go home **ir a casa**
to eat **comer**	to study **estudiar**	to go to bed **irse a la cama**
to drink **beber**	to work **trabajar**	

BREAKFAST | EL DESAYUNO

Breakfast tends to be a light meal for many people in Spain – sometimes no more than a cup of coffee.

VOCABULARY

bread and butter
el pan y la mantequilla

bread and jam
el pan y la mermelada

hot chocolate
el chocolate caliente

to spread
untar

to have breakfast
desayunar

to skip breakfast
no desayunar

YOU SHOULD KNOW…

At around 10 a.m., "la hora del café" (coffee time), many workers will head to nearby eating places for a coffee or juice, and a quick bite to eat – perhaps some toast, churros, or bread with tomatoes.

baguette
la barra de pan

bread and tomatoes
el pan con tomate

bread rolls
los panecillos

buns
los bollos

cereal
los cereales

churros and chocolate
el chocolate con churros

coffee
el café

coffee with milk
el café con leche

croissant
el croissant

jam
la mermelada

muesli
el muesli

muffin
la magdalena

orange juice
el zumo de naranja

tea
el té

toast
la tostada

MAIN MEALS | LAS COMIDAS PRINCIPALES

Lunch is considered to be the most important meal of the day in Spain and will often involve two or three courses. Many businesses close for an hour or two over lunch.

YOU MIGHT SAY...

What's for dinner?
¿Qué hay de cenar?

What time is lunch?
¿A qué hora comemos?

May I have...?
¿Me pondría...?

Can I try it?
¿Puedo probarlo?

I can't eat...
No puedo comer...

I don't like...
No me gusta...

YOU MIGHT HEAR...

We're having ... for dinner.
Vamos a cenar...

Lunch is at midday.
La comida es a mediodía.

Dinner's ready!
¡La cena está lista!

Would you like...?
¿Quieres...?

Is there anything you don't like to eat?
¿Hay algo que no te guste comer?

VOCABULARY

food
la comida

drink
la bebida

lunch
la comida

dinner
la cena

courses
los platos

recipe
la receta

aperitif
el aperitivo

tapas
las tapas

to have lunch
comer

to have dinner
cenar

to eat out
comer fuera

YOU SHOULD KNOW...

Spaniards don't tend to graze between meals, but children will often have an after-school snack, a custom known as "la merienda".

STARTERS

broth
el caldo

butter-bean stew
las judías estofadas

cold meats
los embutidos

lentil stew
el estofado de lentejas

potato salad
la ensaladilla rusa

vegetable soup
la crema de verdura

MAINS

couscous
el cous cous

noodles
los fideos chinos

pasta
la pasta

potatoes
las patatas

rice
el arroz

roast chicken
el pollo asado

salad
la ensalada

sirloin steak
el filete

vegetables
las verduras

CLASSIC SPANISH DISHES

chickpea stew
el cocido madrileño

fabada
la fabada

fried fish
el pescado frito

gazpacho
el gazpacho

hake with salsa verde
la merluza en salsa verde

lamb chops
las chuletitas de cordero

paella
la paella

ratatouille
el pisto

roast lamb
el cordero asado

TAPAS

calamari
los calamares a la romana

croquettes
las croquetas

Galician-style octopus
el pulpo a la gallega

mussels
los mejillones

olives
las aceitunas

potatoes in spicy tomato sauce
las patatas bravas

prawns in garlic sauce
las gambas al ajillo

Serrano ham
el jamón serrano

Spanish omelette
la tortilla de patatas

DESSERTS

almond cake
la tarta de Santiago

cheesecake
la tarta de queso

chocolate cake
la tarta de chocolate

chocolate mousse
el mousse de chocolate

crème brûlée
la crema catalana

crème caramel
el flan

custard (pudding)
las natillas

fried custard slice
la leche frita

ice cream
el helado

meringue
el merengue

rice pudding
el arroz con leche

sorbet
el sorbete

EATING OUT | COMER EN EL RESTAURANTE

Spanish cuisine is popular all over the world. Eating out is a very important part of Spanish culture, whether it's simply going for a drink and some tapas (small dishes), or a full three-course meal.

YOU MIGHT SAY...

I'd like to make a reservation.
Quiero hacer una reserva.

A table for two, please.
Una mesa para dos, por favor.

We're ready to order.
Ya puede tomarnos el pedido.

What would you recommend?
¿Qué recomienda?

What are the specials today?
¿Qué platos especiales tiene hoy?

May I have ..., please?
Quiero tomar ..., por favor.

Are there vegetarian/vegan options?
¿Hay platos vegetarianos / veganos?

I'm allergic to...
Soy alérgico a...

Excuse me, this is cold.
Perdone, esto está frío.

This is not what I ordered.
Esto no es lo que he pedido.

May we have the bill, please?
¿Nos trae la cuenta, por favor?

YOU MIGHT HEAR...

At what time?
¿A qué hora?

For how many people?
¿Para cuántas personas?

Sorry, we're fully booked.
Lo siento, no nos quedan mesas libres.

Would you like anything to drink?
¿Quieren algo de beber?

Are you ready to order?
¿Les puedo tomar ya el pedido?

I would recommend...
Les recomiendo...

The specials today are...
Los platos especiales de hoy son...

Enjoy your meal!
¡Que aproveche!

VOCABULARY

set menu **el menú**	barman/barmaid **el camarero /** **la camarera**	dairy-free **sin lácteos**
daily specials **los platos del día**	vegetarian **vegetariano**	to order **pedir**
tip **la propina**	vegan **vegano**	to book a table **reservar una mesa**
wine waiter **el sumiller /** **la sumiller**	gluten-free **sin gluten**	to ask for the bill **pedir la cuenta**

YOU SHOULD KNOW...

In some Spanish restaurants, there is a cover fee for bread and water. Bread may come accompanied by olive oil to dip bread into, rather than butter as a spread.

bar
el bar

bill
la cuenta

bread basket
la cesta del pan

chair
la silla

champagne flute
la copa alta

cheese knife
el cuchillo del queso

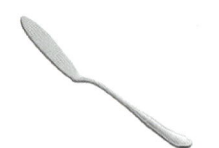

fish knife
el cuchillo de pescado

jug of water
la jarra de agua

menu
el menú

napkin
la servilleta

salt and pepper
la sal y la pimienta

steak knife
el cuchillo para la carne

table
la mesa

tablecloth
el mantel

toothpicks
los palillos de dientes

vinegar and oil
el vinagre y el aceite

waiter/waitress
el camarero / la camarera

wine glass
el vaso de vino

FAST FOOD | LA COMIDA RÁPIDA

Fast food may not be the first thing you think of when it comes to Spanish cuisine, but there are still plenty of options for eating on the go.

YOU MIGHT SAY...

I'd like to order, please.
Quiero hacer un pedido, por favor.

Do you deliver?
¿Entregan a domicilio?

I'm sitting in/taking away.
Para consumir en el establecimiento. / Para llevar.

How long will it be?
¿Cuánto tardará?

That's everything, thanks.
Eso es todo, gracias.

YOU MIGHT HEAR...

Can I help you?
¿Puedo ayudarle?

Sit-in or takeaway?
¿Para consumir en el establecimiento o para llevar?

Small, medium or large?
¿Pequeño, mediano o grande?

We do/don't do delivery.
Entregamos / No entregamos a domicilio.

Would you like anything else?
¿Quiere algo más?

VOCABULARY

fast-food chain
la cadena de comida rápida

food stall
el puesto de comida para llevar

street food market
el mercado de comida callejera

vendor
el vendedor / la vendedora

takeaway food
la comida para llevar

online order
el pedido en línea

an order to go/ a takeaway
un pedido para llevar

delivery charge
los gastos de envío

delivery man/woman
el repartidor / la repartidora

to phone in an order
hacer un pedido por teléfono

to order food
hacer un pedido de comida

to collect an order
recoger un pedido

burger
la hamburguesa

churros and chocolate
el chocolate con churros

filled baguette
el bocadillo

fries
las patatas fritas

hot dog
el perrito caliente

kebab
el pincho moruno

noodles
los fideos chinos

omelette
la tortilla francesa

pizza
la pizza

sandwich
el sándwich

sushi
el sushi

wrap
el wrap

COMMUNICATION AND IT
LA COMUNICACIÓN Y LA INFORMÁTICA

Technology plays a huge role in people's everyday lives. A mere click, tap, or swipe helps us to stay in touch with friends and family, keep up to date with what's going on, and find the information we need.

YOU MIGHT SAY/HEAR

I'll give you a call later.
Te llamo más tarde.

I'll text/email you.
Te enviaré un mensaje / un correo electrónico.

Can you text me?
¿Puedes mandarme un mensaje?

This is a bad line.
No hay buena línea.

I don't have any signal/WiFi.
No tengo conexión / cobertura.

What's your number/email address?
¿Cuál es tu número de teléfono / dirección de correo electrónico?

The website address is…
La dirección de la web es…

What's the WiFi password?
¿Cuál es la contraseña del wifi?

It's all one word.
Se escribe todo junto.

It's upper/lower case.
Es con mayúsculas / minúsculas.

VOCABULARY

post
el mensaje

social media
las redes sociales

email
el correo electrónico

email address
la dirección de correo electrónico

internet
internet

WiFi
wifi

website
la web

link
el enlace

icon
el icono

mouse
el ratón

mouse mat
la alfombrilla del ratón

keyboard
el teclado

app
la aplicación

data
los datos

mobile phone
el teléfono móvil

landline **la línea fija**	screen **la pantalla**	to leave a voice mail **dejar un mensaje de voz**
phone/video call **la llamada telefónica / de vídeo**	button **el botón**	to post (online) **publicar (en línea)**
text message **el mensaje de texto**	battery **la batería**	to download/upload **bajar / subir**
voice mail **el buzón de voz**	cable **el cable**	to charge your phone **cargar el teléfono**
touchscreen **la pantalla táctil**	to make a phone call **hacer una llamada de teléfono**	to switch on/off **encender / apagar**
		to click on **hacer clic en**

YOU SHOULD KNOW...

Spanish computer keyboards use the QWERTY layout – you will find the letter Ñ next to L.

charger
el cargador

computer
el ordenador

SIM card
la tarjeta SIM

smartphone
el teléfono inteligente

tablet
la tableta

wireless router
el router inalámbrico

EDUCATION | LA EDUCACIÓN

Compulsory education in Spain begins at age 6 through to age 16. Nursery schooling is optional, but parents can apply to the local "ayuntamiento" (town hall) to register their child in a state nursery that is provided free of charge.

YOU MIGHT SAY...

What are you studying?
¿Qué estudias?

What year are you in?
¿En qué curso estás?

What's your favourite subject?
¿Cuál es tu asignatura favorita?

Do you have any homework?
¿Tienes deberes?

YOU MIGHT HEAR...

I'm studying...
Estudio...

I'm in Year 6/my final year.
Estoy en sexto / el último curso.

I have an assignment.
Tengo que hacer un trabajo.

VOCABULARY

nursery school
la escuela infantil

primary school
el colegio de primaria

secondary school
el instituto

college
la universidad

university
la universidad

headteacher
el director / la directora

primary school teacher
el maestro / la maestra

secondary school teacher
el profesor / la profesora

pupil
el alumno / la alumna

lesson
la clase

lecture
la conferencia

homework
los deberes

exam
el examen

degree
el título

undergraduate
el estudiante de grado / la estudiante de grado

postgraduate
el estudiante de posgrado / la estudiante de posgrado

classroom
el aula *f*

canteen
el comedor

assembly hall
el salón de actos

playground
el patio

playing field
el campo de juego

halls of residence
la residencia de estudiantes

student union
el sindicato de estudiantes

student card
el carnet de estudiante

to learn
aprender

to teach
enseñar

to revise
repasar

to sit an exam
presentarse a un examen

to graduate
graduarse

to study
estudiar

YOU SHOULD KNOW...

Children attending state schools do not have to wear a school uniform, but religious and private schools generally do have uniform policies.

SCHOOL

colouring pencils
las pinturas

eraser
la goma de borrar

exercise book
el cuaderno de ejercicios

paper
el papel

pen
el bolígrafo

pencil
el lápiz

pencil case
el estuche

ruler
la regla

schoolbag
la mochila escolar

sharpener
el sacapuntas

textbook
el libro de texto

whiteboard
la pizarra

HIGHER EDUCATION

cafeteria
la cafetería

campus
el campus

lecture hall
la sala de conferencias

lecturer
el profesor universitario / la profesora universitaria

library
la biblioteca

student
el estudiante / la estudiante

THE OFFICE | LA OFICINA

Office hours tend to be from 8 a.m. to 6 p.m., with many businesses having a lunch break of 1-2 hours.

YOU MIGHT SAY/HEAR...

Can we arrange a meeting?
¿Podemos fijar una cita?

I have a meeting with...
Tengo una reunión con...

May I ask who's calling?
¿De parte de quién?

I'll email the files to you.
Le enviaré los archivos por correo electrónico.

Can I call you back?
¿Puedo llamarle más tarde?

Mr/Ms ... is on the phone.
El señor / la señora ... está al teléfono.

May I speak to...?
¿Puedo hablar con...?

Here's my business card.
Esta es mi tarjeta de negocios.

YOU SHOULD KNOW...

At lunchtime, eating at one's office desk rather than taking a break with colleagues is seen as unusual, even antisocial, by many Spanish people.

VOCABULARY

manager
el gerente / la gerente

staff
la plantilla

colleague
el compañero / la compañera

client
el cliente / la clienta

human resources
los recursos humanos

accounts
las cuentas

figures
las cifras

spreadsheet
la hoja de cálculo

presentation
la presentación

report
el informe

meeting
la reunión

conference call
la teleconferencia

video conference
la videoconferencia

inbox
la bandeja de entrada

file
el archivo

attachment
el archivo adjunto

username
el nombre de usuario

password
la contraseña

to type
escribir a máquina

to log on/off
acceder al sistema / salir del sistema

to give a presentation
dar una presentación

to hold a meeting
celebrar una reunión

to crash (computer)
bloquearse (el ordenador)

calculator
la calculadora

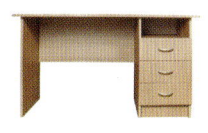

desk
el escritorio

desk lamp
la lámpara de escritorio

filing cabinet
el archivador

folder
la carpeta

hole punch
la taladradora

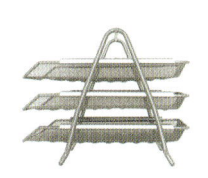

in/out tray
la bandeja de entrada / salida

laptop
el ordenador portátil

notepad
el bloc de notas

paper clip
el clip

photocopier
la fotocopiadora

printer
la impresora

ring binder
la carpeta de anillas

scanner
el escáner

scissors
las tijeras

stapler
la grapadora

sticky notes
las notas adhesivas

sticky tape
el celo

swivel chair
la silla giratoria

telephone
el teléfono

USB stick
la memoria USB

THE BANK | LA BANCA

Most banks are open until 2 p.m. or 2:30 p.m. from Monday to Friday, and some on Saturday mornings, though this can vary.

YOU MIGHT SAY...

I'd like to...
Querría...

... open an account.
... abrir una cuenta.

... apply for a loan/mortgage.
... solicitar un préstamo / una hipoteca.

... register for online banking.
... darme de alta para la banca por internet / online.

Is there a fee for this service?
¿Hay algún recargo por este servicio?

I need to cancel my debit/credit card.
Tengo que cancelar mi tarjeta de débito / crédito.

YOU MIGHT HEAR...

May I see your ID, please?
¿Puedo ver su documento de identidad, por favor?

How much would you like to withdraw/deposit?
¿Cuánto quiere retirar / depositar?

Could you enter your PIN, please?
¿Puede teclear su PIN, por favor?

You must fill out an application form.
Debe rellenar un formulario de solicitud.

You must make an appointment.
Debe concertar una cita.

There is a fee for this service.
Este servicio tiene un recargo.

Is there anything else I can help you with today?
¿Le puedo ayudar en algo más?

VOCABULARY

branch
la sucursal

cashier
el cajero / la cajera

online banking
la banca por internet

bank account
la cuenta bancaria

current account
la cuenta corriente

savings account
la cuenta de ahorros

account number
el número de cuenta

account holder
el titular de la cuenta / la titular de la cuenta

bank statement **el extracto de cuenta**	savings book **la libreta de ahorros**	to borrow **pedir prestado**
bank balance **el saldo**	currency **la moneda**	to repay **devolver el dinero**
overdraft **el descubierto**	loan **el préstamo**	to withdraw **sacar dinero**
bank transfer **la transferencia bancaria**	mortgage **la hipoteca**	to make a deposit **depositar dinero en la cuenta**
chequebook **el talonario de cheques**	interest **el interés**	to change money **cambiar dinero**

YOU SHOULD KNOW…

If using a foreign debit card whilst in Spain, most cash machines will give you the option of carrying out transactions in English.

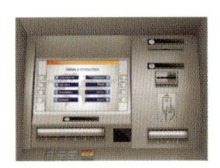

ATM
el cajero automático

banknotes
los billetes de banco

bureau de change
la casa de cambio

debit/credit card
la tarjeta de débito / crédito

exchange rate
el tipo de cambio

safety deposit box
la caja fuerte de seguridad

THE POST OFFICE | LA OFICINA DE CORREOS

Opening hours for post offices will vary from place to place. Certain services – like parcel collection, prepayment, and sending certain official documents – can be requested via the Spanish postal service's website.

YOU MIGHT SAY...

I'd like to send this as special delivery/airmail.
Quiero enviar esto por correo urgente / correo aéreo.

I'd like to drop off a prepaid parcel.
Quiero depositar un paquete de prepago.

Can I get a certificate of postage?
¿Podría darme un comprobante de envío?

I'd like to buy ... stamps, please.
Quisiera comprar ... sellos, por favor.

YOU MIGHT HEAR...

Place it on the scales, please.
Póngalo en la balanza, por favor.

What are the contents?
¿Qué contiene?

What is the value of this parcel?
¿Qué valor tiene el paquete?

You can track the delivery online.
Puede hacer un seguimiento en línea de la entrega.

Would you like a certificate of postage?
¿Quiere un comprobante de envío?

VOCABULARY

address
la dirección

special delivery
el correo urgente

standard post
el correo ordinario

eco box
la caja verde

tracking number
el localizador del envío

courier
el mensajero / la mensajera

mail
el correo

airmail
el correo aéreo

to post
mandar por correo

to send
enviar

YOU SHOULD KNOW...

At Spanish post offices, it is possible to buy "eco boxes" for parcels if you're looking for a more eco-friendly way to send mail.

box
la caja

envelope
el sobre

letter
la carta

package
el paquete

padded envelope
el sobre acolchado

postal worker
**el cartero /
la cartera**

postbox
el buzón

postcard
la postal

stamp
el sello

IN TOWN | EN EL CENTRO

YOU MIGHT SAY...

How do I get to the city centre?
¿Cómo puedo ir al centro de la ciudad?

I'd like to visit...
Me gustaría visitar...

I need to go to...
Necesito ir a...

What are the opening hours?
¿Cuál es el horario de apertura?

YOU MIGHT HEAR...

It's open between ... and...
Abre entre las ... y las...

It's closed on Mondays.
Cierra los lunes.

PLACES OF IMPORTANCE

café
la cafetería

cathedral
la catedral

church
la iglesia

conference centre
el centro de conferencias

courthouse
el juzgado

fire station
el parque de bomberos

fountain
la fuente

hospital
el hospital

hotel
el hotel

laundrette
la lavandería

library
la biblioteca

mosque
la mezquita

office block
el bloque de oficinas

park
el parque

playground
el área de juegos

police station
la comisaría de policía

synagogue
la sinagoga

town hall
el ayuntamiento

LEISURE | EL OCIO

A day trip, a break away, a night out, maybe even a night in – we all like to spend our free time differently. It's also a common topic of conversation with friends and colleagues; who doesn't like talking about holidays, hobbies, and how they like to hang out?

tent
la tienda de campaña

guy rope
el viento

flysheet
el doble techo

groundsheet
el suelo impermeable

tent peg
la estaca

THE BASICS | LO ESENCIAL

YOU MIGHT SAY...

What would you like to do?
¿Qué te gustaría hacer?

What do you do in your spare time?
¿Qué haces en tu tiempo libre?

Have you got any hobbies?
¿Tienes alguna afición?

Do you enjoy...?
¿Te gusta...?

How did you get into...?
¿Qué hizo que te gustara...?

Are you sporty/creative?
¿Eres deportista / creativo?

Are you going on holiday this year?
¿Te vas de vacaciones este año?

YOU MIGHT HEAR...

My hobbies are...
Mis aficiones son...

I like...
Me gusta...

I really enjoy it.
Me gusta mucho.

It's not for me.
No me interesa.

I'm going on holiday.
Me voy de vacaciones.

I am sporty/creative.
Soy deportista / creativo.

I have/don't have a lot of spare time.
Tengo / No tengo mucho tiempo libre.

VOCABULARY

spare time
el tiempo libre

activity
la actividad

hobby/pastime
el pasatiempo

holiday
las vacaciones

passion
la pasión

keen
aficionado

fun
divertido

boring
aburrido

to be interested in
tener interés por

to pass the time
pasar el tiempo

to relax
relajarse

to enjoy
disfrutar

to be bored
aburrirse

cooking
la cocina

DIY
el bricolaje

gaming
los videojuegos

gardening
la jardinería

jogging
correr

listening to music
escuchar música

reading
la lectura

shopping
las compras

sports
los deportes

travelling
viajar

walking
caminar

watching TV/films
ver la tele / ver películas

SIGHTSEEING | EL TURISMO

Spain is one of the most popular tourist destinations in the world: its beautiful scenery and historic cities offer a wealth of sightseeing opportunities to explore.

YOU MIGHT SAY...

How much is it to get in?
¿Cuánto cuesta la entrada?

Is there a discount for students/seniors?
¿Hay descuento para estudiantes / personas mayores?

Where is the tourist office?
¿Dónde está la oficina de turismo?

Are there sightseeing tours?
¿Hay visitas turísticas?

Are there audio guides available?
¿Tienen audioguías?

YOU MIGHT HEAR...

Entry costs...
La entrada cuesta...

There is/isn't a discount available.
Hay / No hay descuento.

The tourist office is located...
La oficina de turismo está...

You can book a guided tour.
Puede reservar una visita guiada.

Audio guides are/are not available.
Tenemos / No tenemos audioguías.

VOCABULARY

tourist
el turista / la turista

tourist attraction
la atracción turística

tourist route
la ruta turística

excursion
la excursión

nature reserve
la reserva natural

historic site
el lugar histórico

audio guide
la audioguía

to visit
visitar

to see
ver

YOU SHOULD KNOW...

Some cultural and historical sites, such as museums, art galleries, and castles, are closed on certain days of the week (often Mondays).

art gallery
el museo de arte

camera
la cámara

castle
el castillo

cathedral
la catedral

city map
el mapa de la ciudad

gardens
los jardines

guidebook
la guía

monument
el monumento

museum
el museo

sightseeing bus
el autobús turístico

tour guide
**el guía turístico /
la guía turística**

tourist office
la oficina de turismo

EVENINGS OUT | POR LA NOCHE

Spaniards love going out in the evenings and the nightlife in many Spanish towns and cities is vibrant and interesting. Check the local tourist office for information on events and venues, and why not get personal recommendations on bars and clubs from residents, too?

YOU MIGHT SAY...

What is there to do at night?
¿Qué se puede hacer aquí por la noche?

What's on at the cinema?
¿Qué ponen en el cine?

Where are the best bars/clubs?
¿Dónde están los mejores bares / las mejores discotecas?

Do you want to go for a drink?
¿Quieres salir a tomar algo?

Do you want to go and see a film/show?
¿Quieres ir a ver una película / un espectáculo?

Are there tickets for...?
¿Quedan entradas para...?

Two seats in the stalls/balcony, please.
Dos entradas para el patio de butacas / la platea, por favor.

What time does it start?
¿A qué hora empieza?

I enjoyed myself.
Me lo he pasado muy bien.

YOU MIGHT HEAR...

The nightlife is/isn't great here.
Hay / No hay mucha vida nocturna por aquí.

My favourite bar/club is...
Mi bar favorito / discoteca favorita es...

I'm going for a few drinks/to the theatre.
Voy a tomar unas copas / al teatro.

I'm going for tapas.
Me voy de tapas.

There's a film/show I'd like to see.
Hay una película / un espectáculo que me gustaría ver.

There are/are no tickets left.
Quedan / No quedan entradas.

It begins at 7 o'clock.
Empieza a las 7 en punto.

Please turn off your mobile phones.
Por favor, apaguen sus teléfonos móviles.

Did you have a good night?
¿Lo has pasado bien esta noche?

VOCABULARY

a drink **una bebida**	play **la obra de teatro**	to order food/drinks **pedir comida / bebidas**
tapas **las tapas**	film **la película**	to see a show **ver un espectáculo**
nightlife **la vida nocturna**	festival **el festival**	to watch a film **ver una película**
party **la fiesta**	box office **la taquilla**	to go dancing **ir a bailar**
show **el espectáculo**	to socialize **hacer vida social**	to enjoy oneself **divertirse**

YOU SHOULD KNOW...

Tapas is an important part of bar culture in Spain. There are lots of different ways to "do tapas": some bars offer a free "tapa" with your drink, in others you can order "tapas" from the menu, while yet others might offer "raciones" (literally "portions") – larger dishes that can be shared between a few people.

ballet
el ballet

bar
el bar

carnival
el carnaval

casino
el casino

cinema
el cine

circus
el circo

comedy show
el espectáculo de humor

concert
el concierto

funfair
la feria

musical
el musical

nightclub
la discoteca

opera
la ópera

restaurant
el restaurante

tapas
las tapas

theatre
el teatro

HOTEL | EL HOTEL

Spain is an extremely popular holiday destination and there's a vast range of accommodation available for visitors, from high-end hotels to cosy and traditional country houses ("casas rurales").

YOU MIGHT SAY...

Have you got rooms available?
¿Tiene habitaciones libres?

How much is it per night?
¿Cuánto cuesta por noche?

Is breakfast included?
¿Incluye el desayuno?

Is there a tourist tax?
¿Hay impuesto turístico?

I'd like to check in/out, please.
Quiero registrarme / dejar la habitación, por favor.

I have a reservation.
Tengo una reserva.

I'd like to book a single/double room, please.
Quiero reservar una habitación individual / doble, por favor.

What time do I have to check out?
¿A qué hora tengo que dejar la habitación?

What time is breakfast served?
¿A qué hora se sirve el desayuno?

I'm in room number...
Mi habitación es la...

I need fresh towels/more soap for my room.
Necesito toallas limpias / más jabón para mi habitación.

I've lost my key.
He perdido la llave.

I'd like to make a complaint.
Quiero presentar una reclamación.

YOU SHOULD KNOW...

When checking in to your hotel, you are expected to fill out a registration form ("la tarjeta de registro") and provide your passport number. In some parts of Spain, in particular the Balearic Islands, a tourist tax is payable per person, per night. The amount depends on how you long you are staying.

YOU MIGHT HEAR...

We have/don't have rooms available.
Tenemos / No nos quedan habitaciones libres.

Breakfast is/is not included.
El desayuno está / no está incluido.

Our rates are...
El precio es...

Breakfast is served at...
El desayuno se sirve a las...

May I have your room number?
¿Me dice el número de su habitación?

You may check in after...
La habitación estará disponible para usted después de las...

May I see your passport, please?
¿Puedo ver su pasaporte, por favor?

You must check out before...
Tiene que dejar la habitación antes de las...

VOCABULARY

bed and breakfast
el alojamiento y desayuno

full board
la pensión completa

half board
la media pensión

room service
el servicio de habitaciones

wake-up call
la llamada despertador

room number
el número de habitación

per person per night
por persona y noche

tourist tax
el impuesto turístico

to check in
registrarse

to check out
dejar la habitación

to order room service
pedir el servicio de habitaciones

corridor
el pasillo

"do not disturb" sign
el cartel de "no molestar"

double room
la habitación doble

key card
la llave de tarjeta

minibar
el minibar

porter
el mozo / la moza

reception
la recepción

receptionist
el recepcionista / la receptionista

safe
la caja fuerte

single room
la habitación individual

toiletries
los artículos de perfumería

twin room
la habitación de dos camas

CAMPING | EL CAMPING

There are numerous campsites in Spain, offering different types of accommodation and facilities for travellers. There are also options for wild camping ("acampada libre"), but check what the local and national restrictions are before you set off on your trip.

YOU MIGHT SAY...

Have you got spaces available?
¿Tiene plazas libres?

Is it OK to camp here?
¿Está permitido acampar aquí?

I'd like to book for ... nights.
Quiero reservar para ... noches.

How much is it per night?
¿Cuánto cuesta por noche?

Where is the toilet/shower block?
¿Dónde están los aseos / las duchas?

Is the water drinkable?
¿Es potable el agua?

YOU MIGHT HEAR...

You can/can't put your tent up here.
Puedes / No puedes levantar la tienda aquí.

We have spaces available.
Tenemos plazas libres.

We don't have spaces available.
No tenemos plazas libres.

It costs ... per night.
Cuesta ... por noche.

The toilets/showers are located...
Los aseos / Las duchas están...

The water is/is not drinkable.
El agua es / no es potable.

VOCABULARY

campsite
el camping

chalet
la cabaña

pitch
la parcela

electricity hook-up
el cable conector

toilet/shower block
el bloque de los aseos / las duchas

rubbish bins
los cubos de basura

camper
el campista / la campista

to camp
acampar

to pitch a tent
montar una tienda

to take down a tent
desmontar una tienda

to go caravanning
viajar en caravana

air bed
la colchoneta inflable

camping stove
el hornillo de gas

caravan
la caravana

cool box
la nevera de camping

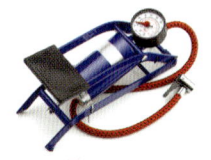

footpump
la bomba de pie

mat
la esterilla

matches
las cerillas

motorhome
la autocaravana

rucksack
la mochila

sleeping bag
el saco de dormir

tent
la tienda de campaña

torch
la linterna

THE BEACH | LA PLAYA

Spain has over 3,700 miles of varying coastline: the sandy beaches of the Mediterranean are always popular with holidaymakers; the Costa Brava, in the north of Catalonia, is wild and rugged; and the northern coasts of Asturias and the Basque Country are great for surfing.

YOU MIGHT SAY...

Is there a good beach nearby?
¿Hay alguna playa buena cerca?

Is swimming permitted here?
¿Está permitido nadar aquí?

Is the water cold?
¿Está fría el agua?

Can we hire...?
¿Podemos alquilar...?

Help! Lifeguard!
¡Ayuda! ¡Socorrista!

YOU MIGHT HEAR...

This is a public/private beach.
Esta es una playa pública / privada.

Swimming is allowed/forbidden.
Está permitido / No está permitido nadar.

Swimming is/is not supervised.
La playa tiene / no tiene socorrista.

The water is warm/cold/freezing!
El agua está templada / fría / helada.

VOCABULARY

"No swimming."	lifeguard station	to sunbathe
"Prohibido nadar."	el puesto de socorrista	tomar el sol
bathing zone	suntan	to swim
la zona de baño	el moreno	nadar

YOU SHOULD KNOW...

Public beaches are often monitored and may use a flag system to indicate bathing conditions:
Green – "bathing permitted and monitored"
Orange – "bathing permitted and monitored, but not recommended"
Red – "bathing forbidden and unmonitored".

THE SEASIDE

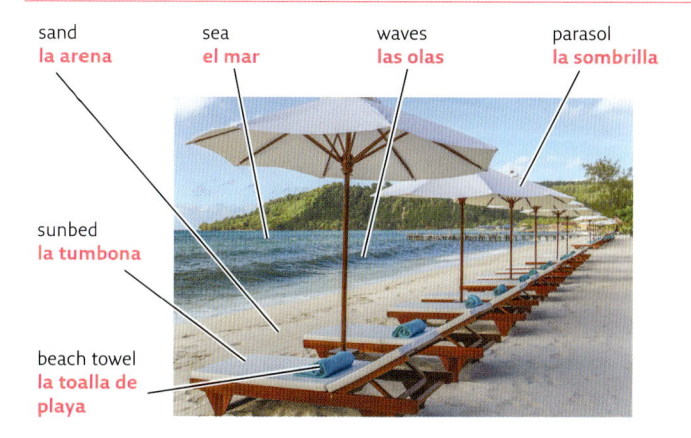

- sand — **la arena**
- sea — **el mar**
- waves — **las olas**
- parasol — **la sombrilla**
- sunbed — **la tumbona**
- beach towel — **la toalla de playa**

GENERAL

beach ball
la pelota de playa

beach tent
la tienda de playa

bikini
el bikini

bucket and spade
el cubo y la pala

deck chair
la tumbona

flip-flops
las chanclas

flippers
las aletas

promenade
el paseo marítimo

rubber ring
el flotador

sandcastle
el castillo de arena

seashells
las conchas

seaweed
el alga marina *f*

snorkel
la máscara y el tubo de buceo

sunglasses
las gafas de sol

sunhat
el sombrero para el sol

suntan lotion
la loción bronceadora

swimming trunks
el bañador

swimsuit
el traje de baño

156

MUSIC | LA MÚSICA

Spain plays host to a huge variety of music festivals over the summer months, from large-scale pop and rock concerts to local traditional music events.

YOU MIGHT SAY...

I enjoy listening to music.
Me gusta escuchar música.

I play the...
Toco el / la...

I'm learning to play...
Estoy aprendiendo a tocar...

What kind of music do you like?
¿Qué estilo de música te gusta?

Is there a live music scene here?
¿Hay buen ambiente musical por aquí?

YOU MIGHT HEAR...

My favourite group is...
Mi grupo favorito es...

There's a good music scene here.
Hay muy buen ambiente musical por aquí.

VOCABULARY

CD
el CD

vinyl record
el disco de vinilo

album
el álbum

microphone
el micrófono

song
la canción

band
el grup

live music
la música en directo

singer-songwriter
el cantautor / la cantautora

gig
el concierto

pop
el pop

rock
el rock

hip-hop
el hip-hop

rap
el rap

classical
la música clásica

folk
el folk

to play an instrument
tocar un instrumento

to sing
cantar

to listen to music
escuchar música

to go to gigs
ir a conciertos

to stream music
escuchar música en streaming

EQUIPMENT

Bluetooth® speaker
el altavoz de Bluetooth®

earphones
los auriculares

headphones
los auriculares

soundbar
la barra de sonido

speakers
los altavoces

turntable
el plato

MUSICAL INSTRUMENTS

accordion
el acordeón

acoustic guitar
la guitarra acústica

bass drum
el bombo

bass guitar
el bajo

cello
el violoncelo

clarinet
el clarinete

cymbals
los platillos

double bass
el contrabajo

electric guitar
la guitarra eléctrica

flute
la flauta travesera

harp
el arpa *f*

keyboard
el teclado

mouth organ
la armónica

piano
el piano

saxophone
el saxofón

snare drum
la caja

trombone
el trombón

trumpet
la trompeta

159

tuba
el tuba

violin
el violín

xylophone
el xilófono

GENERAL

backing group
el grupo de acompañamiento

choir
el coro

conductor
el director / la directora

DJ
el DJ / la DJ

musician
el músico / la música

music stand
el atril

orchestra
la orquesta

sheet music
las hojas de partitura

singer
el cantante / la cantante

PHOTOGRAPHY | LA FOTOGRAFÍA

YOU MIGHT SAY...

Can I take photos here?
¿Puedo sacar fotos aquí?

Where can I print my photos?
¿Dónde puedo imprimir mis fotos?

YOU MIGHT HEAR...

Photography isn't allowed.
Sacar fotos no está permitido.

Say cheese!
¡Sonría! / ¡Sonrían!

VOCABULARY

photo
la foto

photographer
el fotógrafo / la fotógrafa

selfie
el selfi

selfie stick
el paloselfi

to take a photo/selfie
tomar una foto / un selfi

to zoom in
aumentar

camera lens
el objetivo de la cámara

compact camera
la cámara compacta

drone
el dron

DSLR camera
la cámara DSLR

SD card
la tarjeta de memoria

tripod
el trípode

GAMES | LOS JUEGOS

Board game cafés where you can get together over a drink and a favourite board game make for great opportunities to use and improve your Spanish!

YOU MIGHT SAY...

Shall we play a game?
¿Jugamos a algo?

What would you like to play?
¿A qué te gustaría jugar?

What are the rules?
¿Cuáles son las reglas?

YOU MIGHT HEAR...

It's your turn.
Te toca a ti.

Time's up!
Se ha acabado el tiempo.

Shall we play something else?
¿Jugamos a otra cosa?

VOCABULARY

player
el jugador / la jugadora

charades
el juego de charadas

hide and seek
el escondite

solitaire
el solitario

poker
el póquer

hand (in cards)
la mano

video game
el videojuego

games console
la consola de videojuegos

game controller
el mando de juego

joystick
el joystick

virtual reality headset
las gafas de realidad virtual

to play
jugar

to roll the dice
tirar el dado / los dados

to win
ganar

to lose
perder

YOU SHOULD KNOW...

A traditional Spanish deck of cards can be used for some games. This deck consists of four suits ("palos"): "oros" (gold coins), "copas" (cups), "espadas" (swords), and "bastos" (clubs). A popular card game is "mus" – the aim is for you and a partner to try and trick an opposing pair of players.

board game **el juego de mesa**	bowling **los bolos**	cards **las cartas**
chess **el ajedrez**	counters **las fichas**	crossword **el crucigrama**
darts **los dardos**	dice **los dados**	dominoes **el dominó**
draughts **las damas**	jigsaw puzzle **el puzzle**	ludo **el parchís**

ARTS AND CRAFTS | LAS ARTESANÍAS

It is easy to find samples of traditional Spanish crafts such as ceramics, glassware or "marroquinería" (leather goods) in specialist shops, markets, or craft fairs. Some traditional workshops offer guided visits and even classes.

VOCABULARY

handicrafts
las manualidades

craft fair
la feria de artesanía

artist
el artista / la artista

amateur
el aficionado / la aficionada

dressmaker
el costurero / la costurera

cardboard
la cartulina

glue
el pegamento

to paint
pintar

to sketch
bosquejar

to sew
coser

to knit
hacer punto

to be creative
ser creativo

GENERAL CRAFTS

embroidery
el bordado

jewellery-making
la fabricación de joyas

model-making
el modelismo

papercrafts
las manualidades de papel

pottery
la cerámica

woodwork
la carpintería

ART MATERIALS

canvas
el lienzo

easel
el caballete

ink
la tinta

oil paint
la pintura al óleo

paintbrush
el pincel

palette
la paleta

paper
el papel

pastels
los pasteles

pen
el bolígrafo

pencil
el lápiz

sketchpad
el cuaderno de bocetos

watercolours
las acuarelas

SEWING ACCESSORIES

ball of wool
el ovillo de lana

buttons
los botones

crochet hook
la aguja de ganchillo

fabric
la tela

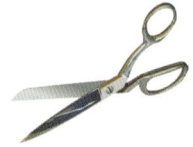

fabric scissors
las tijeras de tela

knitting needles
las agujas de hacer punto

needle and thread
la aguja y el hilo

pins
los alfileres

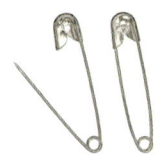

safety pin
el imperdible

sewing basket
la cesta de la costura

sewing machine
la máquina de coser

tape measure
la cinta métrica

SPORT | EL DEPORTE

Be it football or basketball, cycling or tennis, Spain has an impressive sporting history. There are hundreds of sports and fitness clubs, plus events across the country that you can get involved with, either as a player or as a spectator. You may be looking to participate in a sport, or head to the gym, or you may simply want to chat about how "la Roja" are getting on.

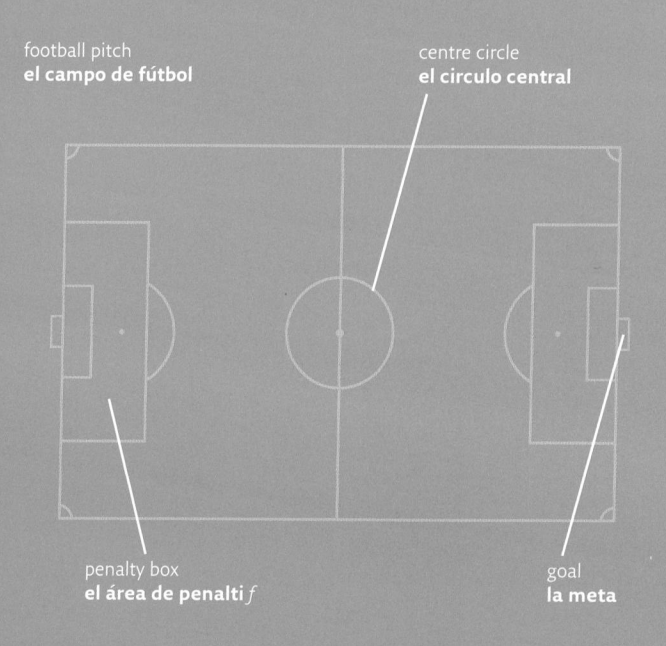

football pitch
el campo de fútbol

centre circle
el circulo central

penalty box
el área de penalti *f*

goal
la meta

THE BASICS | LO ESENCIAL

YOU MIGHT SAY...

I like keeping active.
Me gusta mantenerme activo.

Where is the nearest...?
¿Dónde está el ... más cercano / la ... más cercana?

I train ... times per week.
Hago ejercicio ... veces por semana.

I play rugby/hockey.
Juego al rugby / al hockey.

I'd like to book...
Quiero reservar...

YOU MIGHT HEAR...

Do you play any sports?
¿Practicas algún deporte?

Where/When do you train?
¿Cuándo / Dónde haces ejercicio?

Do you follow any sports?
¿Eres aficionado de algún deporte?

Who's your favourite team/player?
¿Cuál es tu equipo / jugador favorito?

I'm a fan of...
Soy hincha de...

VOCABULARY

tournament
el torneo

competition
la competición

league
la liga

champion
el campeón / la campeona

teammate
el compañero de equipo / la compañera de equipo

competitor
el participante / la participante

coach
el entrenador / la entrenadora

manager
el técnico / la técnica

match
el partido

points
los puntos

to coach
entrenar

to compete
competir

to score
marcar

to win
ganar

to lose
perder

to draw
empatar

leisure centre
el centro deportivo

medal
la medalla

official
el oficial / la oficial

podium
el podio

referee
el árbitro / la árbitra

scoreboard
el marcador

spectators
los espectadores

sportsperson
el deportista / la deportista

stadium
el estadio

stands
las gradas

team
el equipo

trophy
el trofeo

WELLBEING | EL BIENESTAR

YOU MIGHT SAY...

I'd like to join the gym.
Quiero apuntarme al gimnasio.

I'd like to book a class.
Quiero reservar una clase.

What are the facilities like?
¿Cómo son las instalaciones?

What kinds of classes can you do here?
¿Qué tipo de clases ofrecen?

YOU MIGHT HEAR...

Are you a member here?
¿Eres socio de aquí?

Would you like to book an induction?
¿Quiere reservar una clase de introducción?

What time would you like to book for?
¿Para qué hora quiere reservar?

VOCABULARY

gym
el gimnasio

gym instructor
el instructor de gimnasio / la instructora de gimnasio

gym membership
la afiliación al gimnasio

personal trainer
el entrenador personal / la entrenadora personal

exercise class
la clase de fitness

pilates
el Pilates

yoga
el yoga

press-ups
las flexiones

sit-ups
los abdominales

running
el running

running club
el club de running

to exercise
hacer ejercicio

to keep fit
mantenerse en forma

to go for a run
ir a correr

to go to the gym
ir al gimnasio

YOU SHOULD KNOW...

Some gyms may expect you to continue paying for the duration of your membership even if you are unable to continue attending.

THE GYM

changing room
los vestuarios

cross trainer
la bicicleta elíptica

dumbbells
las mancuernas

exercise bike
la bicicleta estática

gym ball
la pelota suiza

kettle bell
la pesa rusa

locker
la taquilla

rowing machine
la máquina de remo

showers
las duchas

skipping rope
la cuerda de saltar

treadmill
la cinta de correr

weightlifting bench
el banco de pesas

FOOTBALL | EL FÚTBOL

Football is the most widely played sport in Spain and it has a huge following. The national team have been World Cup and European champions.

YOU MIGHT SAY...

Are you going to watch the match?
¿Vas a ver el partido?

What's the score?
¿Cómo va el marcador?

That was a foul!
¡Eso ha sido falta!

YOU MIGHT HEAR...

I'm watching the match.
Estoy viendo el partido.

The score is...
La puntuación es...

Go on!
¡Venga!

VOCABULARY

defender
**el defensa /
la defensa**

striker
**el delantero /
la delantera**

substitute
**el suplente /
la suplente**

kick-off
el saque inicial

half-time
el descanso

full-time
el final del partido

extra time
la prórroga

added time
el tiempo añadido

free kick
el tiro libre

header
el cabezazo

save
la parada

foul
la falta

offside
en fuera de juego

penalty kick
el penalti

penalty box
el área de penalti *f*

to play football
jugar al fútbol

to kick
chutar

to tackle
entrar a

to pass the ball
pasar la pelota

to score a goal
marcar un gol

assistant referee
el juez de línea / la juez de línea

football
la pelota de fútbol

football boots
las botas de fútbol

football match
el partido de fútbol

football pitch
el campo de fútbol

football player
el jugador de fútbol / la jugadora de fútbol

goal
la meta

goalkeeper
el portero / la portera

goalkeeper's gloves
los guantes de portero

shin pads
las espinilleras

whistle
el silbato

yellow/red card
la tarjeta amarilla / roja

RUGBY | EL RUGBY

Rugby is not as widely played in Spain as it is in other European countries, but it is gaining in popularity.

VOCABULARY

rugby league/union
el rugby league / union

forward
el delantero / la delantera

back
el zaguero / la zaguera

try
el ensayo

conversion
la conversión

penalty kick
el penalti

drop goal
el drop goal

pass
el pase

tackle
el placaje

headguard
el casco (de rugby)

mouthguard
el protector bucal

to play rugby
jugar al rugby

to tackle
placar

to score a try
marcar un ensayo

rugby
el rugby

rugby ball
la pelota de rugby

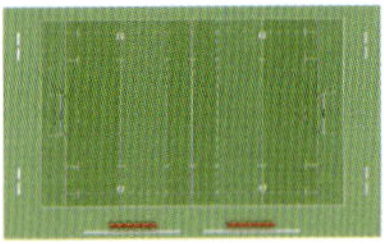

rugby field
el campo de rugby

rugby goalposts
los postes de rugby

rugby player
el jugador de rugby / la jugadora de rugby

scrum
la melé

BASKETBALL | EL BALONCESTO

Basketball is widely played and watched in Spain. The sport has a lively professional league, and the national teams in both basketball and wheelchair basketball have had international success.

VOCABULARY

wheelchair basketball
el baloncesto en silla de ruedas

centre
el pívot / la pívot

layup
la bandeja

slam dunk
el mate

free throw
el tiro libre

hook shot
el gancho

to play basketball
jugar al baloncesto

to catch
agarrar

to throw
lanzar

to dribble
driblar

to block
bloquear

to mark a player
marcar a un jugador

basket
la canasta

basketball
la pelota de baloncesto

basketball court
la cancha de baloncesto

basketball game
el partido de baloncesto

basketball player
el jugador / la jugadora de baloncesto

basketball shoes
las zapatillas de baloncesto

175

RACKET SPORTS | LOS DEPORTES DE RAQUETA

VOCABULARY

ace
el ace

serve
el servicio

backhand
el revés

forehand
el drive

fault
la falta

net
la red

rally
el intercambio

game, set and match
juego, set y partido

singles
sencillos

doubles
dobles

top seed
el primera cabeza / la primera cabeza

to play tennis
jugar al tenis

to play badminton/squash
jugar al bádminton / squash

to hit
golpear

to serve
sacar

to break someone's serve
romper el saque de alguien

BADMINTON

badminton
el bádminton

badminton racket
la raqueta de bádminton

shuttlecock
el volante

SQUASH

squash
el squash

squash ball
la pelota de squash

squash racket
la raqueta de squash

TENNIS

ball boy/girl
el recogepelotas / la recogepelotas

line judge
el juez de línea / la juez de línea

tennis
el tenis

tennis ball
la pelota de tenis

tennis court
la pista de tenis

tennis player
el tenista / la tenista

tennis racket
la raqueta de tenis

umpire
el árbitro / la árbitra

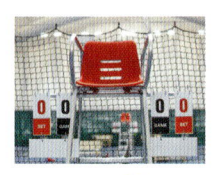

umpire's chair
la silla del árbitro

177

WATER SPORTS | LOS DEPORTES AQUÁTICOS

With its long, varied coastline and plenty of rivers and lakes inland, there is a whole range of water sports you can try out during your time in Spain.

YOU MIGHT SAY...

I'm a keen swimmer.
Me gusta mucho nadar.

I'm not a strong swimmer.
No se me da bien nadar.

Can I hire...?
¿Puedo alquilar...?

YOU MIGHT HEAR...

You can hire...
Puede alquilar...

You must wear a lifejacket.
Debe usar un chaleco salvavidas.

The water is deep/shallow.
El agua es profunda / poca profunda.

VOCABULARY

swimming
la natación

breaststroke
la braza

backstroke
la espalda

front crawl
el crol

butterfly
la mariposa

lane
el carril

length
el largo

swimming lesson
la clase de natación

swimmer
el nadador / la nadadora

diver
el saltador de trampolín / la saltadora de trampolín

diving
el salto de trampolín

angling
la pesca con caña

angler
el pescador / la pescadora

surfer
el surfista / la surfista

to swim
nadar

to dive
saltar

to scuba-dive
hacer buceo

to surf
hacer surf

to paddle
remar

to row
remar

to sail
navegar

to fish
pescar

POOL

armbands
los manguitos

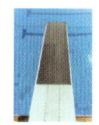

diving board
el trampolín

flippers
las aletas

goggles
las gafas de natación

lifeguard
el socorrista / la socorrista

swimming cap
el gorro

swimming pool
la piscina

swimming trunks
el bañador

swimsuit
el traje de baño

OPEN WATER

bodyboarding
el bodyboarding

canoeing
el piragüismo

jet ski
la moto de agua

kayaking
el kayak

lifejacket
el chaleco salvavidas

oars
los remos

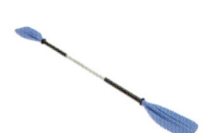

paddle
el remo de kayak

paddleboarding
el stand up

scuba diving
el submarinismo

snorkelling
el buceo con tubo

surfboard
la tabla de surf

surfing
el surfing

waterskiing
el esquí acuático

wetsuit
el traje de neopreno

windsurfing
el windsurf

WINTER SPORTS | LOS DEPORTES DE INVIERNO

There are plenty of places to practise mountain and winter sports in Spain, from the Pyrenees and Picos de Europa in the north, to the Cordillera Central and the Sierra Nevada in the centre and to the south. In spring, you might even be able to sunbathe in the morning and ski in the afternoon!

YOU MIGHT SAY...

How much is the ski pass?
¿Cuál es la tarifa del forfait?

Can I hire some skis?
¿Puedo alquilar unos esquís?

I'd like a skiing lesson, please.
Quiero una clase de esquí, por favor.

I can't ski very well.
No sé esquiar bien.

What are the snow conditions like?
¿Qué condiciones de nieve hay?

I've fallen.
Me he caído.

I've hurt myself.
Me he hecho daño.

YOU MIGHT HEAR...

You can hire skis here.
Puede alquilar los esquís aquí.

You can book a skiing lesson here.
Puede reservar aquí su clase de esquí.

Do you have much skiing experience?
¿Tiene mucha experiencia esquiando?

The piste is open/closed today.
La pista está abierta / cerrada hoy.

The conditions are good/bad.
Las condiciones son buenas / malas.

There's an avalanche risk.
Hay riesgo de avalancha.

VOCABULARY

skier
el esquiador / la esquiadora

ski resort
la estación de esquí

ski instructor
el monitor de esquí / la monitora de esquí

ski pass
el forfait

ski lift
el telesquí

mountain rescue service
el servicio de rescate de montaña

first-aid kit **el botiquín**	avalanche **la avalancha**	to go sledging **ir en trineo**
snow **la nieve**	to ski (off-piste) **esquiar (fuera de pista)**	to go ice skating **ir a patinar sobre hielo**
powder **el polvo**	to snowboard **practicar snowboard**	to go mountain climbing **hacer alpinismo**
ice **el hielo**		

YOU SHOULD KNOW...

If you are planning to try skiing off-piste, it's a good idea to have a guide accompany you, to take a geolocation device with you, and to check beforehand if there is a risk of avalanche. There are also lessons available in many resorts for those who wish to try off-piste skiing.

GENERAL

crampons
los crampones

ice axe
el piolet

ice skates
los patines de hielo

ice skating
el patinaje sobre hielo

rope
la cuerda

sledge
el trineo

SKIING AND SNOWBOARDING

piste
la pista

salopettes
el peto de esquí

ski boots
las botas de esquí

ski gloves
los guantes de esquí

ski goggles
las gafas de esquí

ski helmet
el casco

ski jacket
la chaqueta de esquí

ski poles
los bastones de esquí

skis
los esquís

ski suit
el traje de esquí

snowboard
la tabla de snowboard

snowboarding boots
las botas de snowboard

COMBAT SPORTS | LOS DEPORTES DE COMBATE

VOCABULARY

fight
la pelea

boxer
**el boxeador /
la boxeadora**

fighter/wrestler
**el luchador /
la luchadora**

opponent
**el contrincante /
la contrincante**

featherweight
el peso ligero

heavyweight
el peso pesado

punch
el puñetazo

knockout
el K.O.

martial arts
las artes marciales

to box
boxear

to wrestle
luchar

to punch
dar un puñetazo

to kick
dar una patada

to strike
golpear

to spar
entrenarse

to fence
practicar esgrima

to knock out
dejar K.O.

BOXING

boxing gloves
los guantes de boxeo

boxing ring
el cuadrilátero de boxeo

boxing shoes
las zapatillas de boxeo

headguard
el casco

mouthguard
el protector bucal

punchbag
el saco de boxeo

OTHER COMBAT SPORTS

fencing
la esgrima

judo
el yudo

karate
el kárate

kickboxing
el kickboxing

kung fu
el kung fu

taekwondo
el taekwondo

wrestling
la lucha libre

ATHLETICS | EL ATLETISMO

VOCABULARY

runner
**el corredor /
la corredora**

race
la carrera

marathon
el maratón

sprint
el esprint

lane
la calle

start line
la línea de salida

finish line
la línea de llegada

heat
la prueba

final
la final

triple jump
el triple salto

heptathlon
el heptatlón

decathlon
el decatlón

starter's gun
el disparo de salida

to do athletics
hacer atletismo

to run
correr

to race
echar una carrera

to jump
saltar

to throw
lanzar

athlete
el atleta / la atleta

discus
el lanzamiento de disco

high jump
el salto de altura

hurdles
la carrera de vallas

javelin
la jabalina

long jump
el salto de longitud

pole vault
el salto con pértiga

relay
la carrera de relevos

running track
la pista de atletismo

shot put
el lanzamiento de peso

starting blocks
los tacos de salida

stopwatch
el cronómetro

track shoes
las zapatillas para pista de atletismo

GOLF | EL GOLF

There are golf courses and clubs all over Spain. Golfing holidays are becoming increasingly popular, and you can hire any equipment you may need.

VOCABULARY

golfer
el golfista / la golfista

caddie
el caddie / la caddie

golf course
el campo de golf

fairway
la calle

green
el green

bunker
el búnker

hole
el hoyo

clubhouse
la casa club

swing
el swing

birdie
el birdie

handicap
el hándicap

over/under par
sobre / bajo par

to play golf
jugar al golf

to tee off
dar el primer golpe

golf bag
la bolsa de golf

golf ball
la pelota de golf

golf buggy
el carrito de golf

golf club
el palo de golf

putter
el putter

tee
el tee

OTHER SPORTS | OTROS DEPORTES

American football
el fútbol americano

archery
el tiro al arco

baseball
el béisbol

carom billiards
la carambola

climbing
la escalada

fishing
la pesca

gymnastics
la gimnasia

handball
el balonmano

hockey
el hockey

horse racing
las carreras de caballos

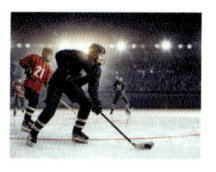

ice hockey
el hockey sobre hielo

motorcycle racing
las carreras de motociclismo

motor racing
las carreras automovilísticas

netball
el netball

petanque
la petanca

shooting
el tiro

showjumping
los concursos de saltos

skateboarding
el patinaje en monopatín

snooker
el snooker

table tennis
el tenis de mesa

track cycling
el ciclismo en pista

volleyball
el voleibol

water polo
el waterpolo

weightlifting
la halterofilia

HEALTH | LA SALUD

It's important to arrange appropriate cover for healthcare during your time in Spain. Healthcare for residents is funded through taxes and provided by a system of public and private hospitals, doctors, and medical professionals. The management of health services is decentralized and run by the autonomous regions ("comunidades autónomas") that make up the Spanish territory, but you can be treated at any hospital in Spain regardless of where you are registered as a patient.

first-aid kit
el botiquín de primeros auxilios

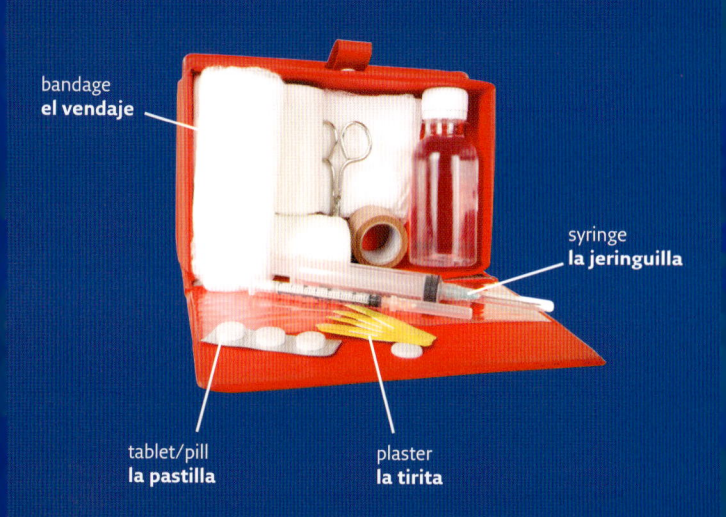

bandage
el vendaje

syringe
la jeringuilla

tablet/pill
la pastilla

plaster
la tirita

THE BASICS | LO ESENCIAL

112 is the Universal European Emergency Services number – it works from all phones, including mobiles, and will connect you to the appropriate emergency service. Other numbers for emergency services in Spain are as follows: 062 – Guardia Civil (police for rural areas, highways and ports); 091 – Policía (police for urban areas); 080 or 085 – Bomberos (fire brigade).

YOU MIGHT SAY...

I don't feel well.
No me siento bien.

I'm going to be sick.
Voy a vomitar.

I need to see a doctor/go to hospital.
Necesito ver a un médico / ir al hospital.

Call an ambulance.
Llame a una ambulancia.

YOU MIGHT HEAR...

What's wrong?
¿Qué le pasa?

Where does it hurt?
¿Dónde le duele?

What happened?
¿Qué ha pasado?

How long have you been feeling ill?
¿Cuánto hace que no se encuentra bien?

YOU SHOULD KNOW...

The "Tarjeta Sanitaria" is the national health insurance card. Although issued by the regional government, it is valid across the whole of the Spanish territory. All Spanish citizens and foreigners with legal residence are entitled to this card – if you intend to obtain one, seek advice on the documentation you will need and the processes to follow.

VOCABULARY

first aider
el socorrista / la socorrista

pain
el dolor

illness
la enfermedad

symptom
el síntoma

mental health
la salud mental

treatment
el tratamiento

recovery
la recuperación

health insurance
el seguro médico

healthy
sano

to be unwell
estar malo

to recover
recuperarse

to look after
cuidar

to treat
tratar

doctor
**el médico /
la médica**

first-aid kit
**el botiquín de
primeros auxilios**

hospital
el hospital

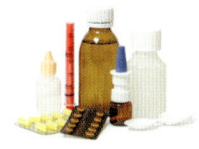

medicine
la medicina

nurse
**el enfermero /
la enfermera**

paramedic
**el paramédico /
la paramédica**

patient
**el paciente /
la paciente**

pharmacist
**el farmacéutico /
la farmacéutica**

pharmacy
la farmacia

THE BODY | EL CUERPO

VOCABULARY

throat **la garganta**	temple **la sien**	sense of touch **el tacto**
armpit **la axila**	skin **la piel**	balance **el equilibrio**
genitals **los genitales**	(body) hair **el vello (corporal)**	to see **ver**
breast **el pecho**	height **la altura**	to smell **oler**
eyelash **la pestaña**	weight **el peso**	to hear **oír**
eyebrow **la ceja**	BMI **el IMC**	to touch **tocar**
eyelid **el párpado**	sense of hearing **el oído**	to taste **notar el sabor de**
earlobe **el lóbulo de la oreja**	sense of sight **la vista**	to stand **estar de pie**
nostrils **los orificios nasales**	sense of smell **el olfato**	to walk **andar**
lips **los labios**	sense of taste **el gusto**	to lose one's balance **perder el equilibrio**

YOU SHOULD KNOW…

In Spanish, possessive adjectives (for example, *my*, *his*, *their*) are not used to refer to one's body parts; reflexive verbs are used instead. For instance, "I washed my hands" is translated as "Me lavé las manos".

FACE

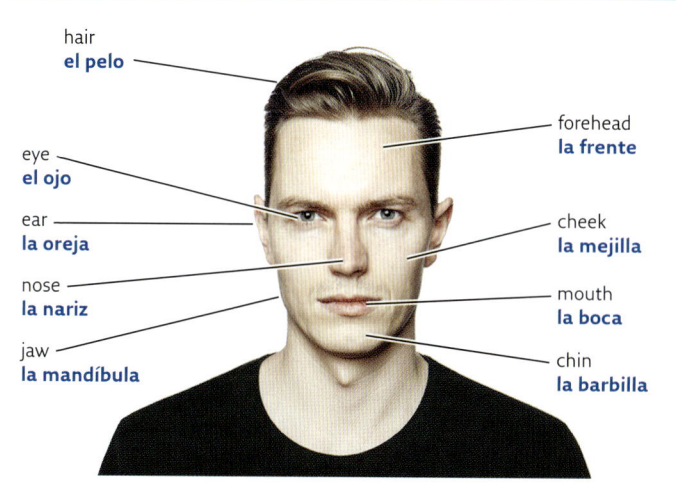

- hair — **el pelo**
- forehead — **la frente**
- eye — **el ojo**
- ear — **la oreja**
- cheek — **la mejilla**
- nose — **la nariz**
- mouth — **la boca**
- jaw — **la mandíbula**
- chin — **la barbilla**

HAND

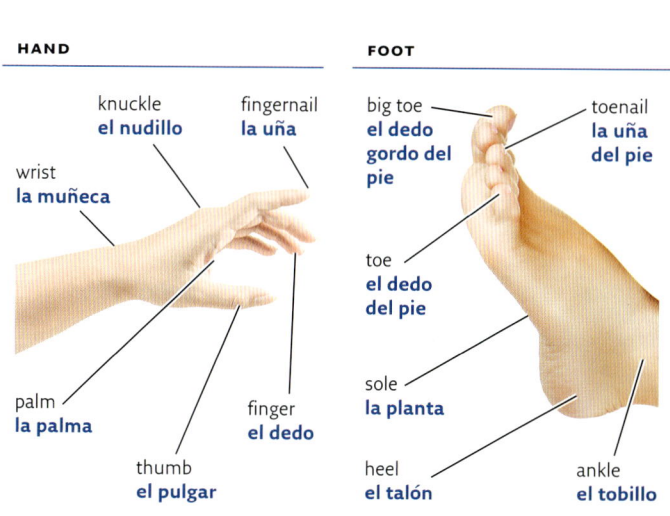

- knuckle — **el nudillo**
- fingernail — **la uña**
- wrist — **la muñeca**
- palm — **la palma**
- thumb — **el pulgar**
- finger — **el dedo**

FOOT

- big toe — **el dedo gordo del pie**
- toenail — **la uña del pie**
- toe — **el dedo del pie**
- sole — **la planta**
- heel — **el talón**
- ankle — **el tobillo**

BODY - FRONT

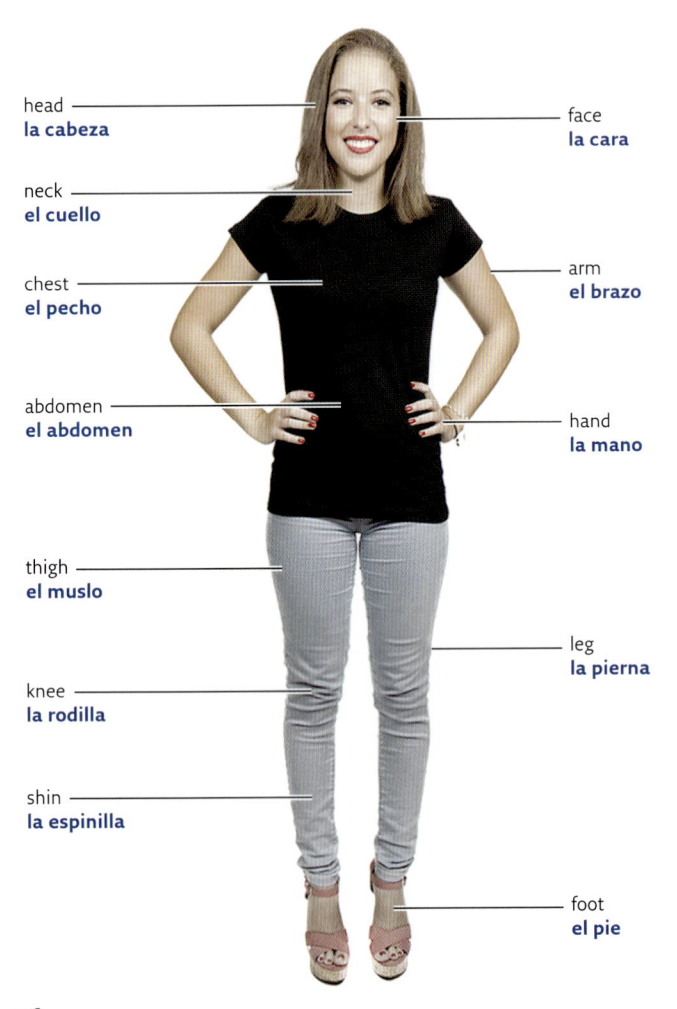

head — **la cabeza**

face — **la cara**

neck — **el cuello**

chest — **el pecho**

arm — **el brazo**

abdomen — **el abdomen**

hand — **la mano**

thigh — **el muslo**

leg — **la pierna**

knee — **la rodilla**

shin — **la espinilla**

foot — **el pie**

BODY – BACK

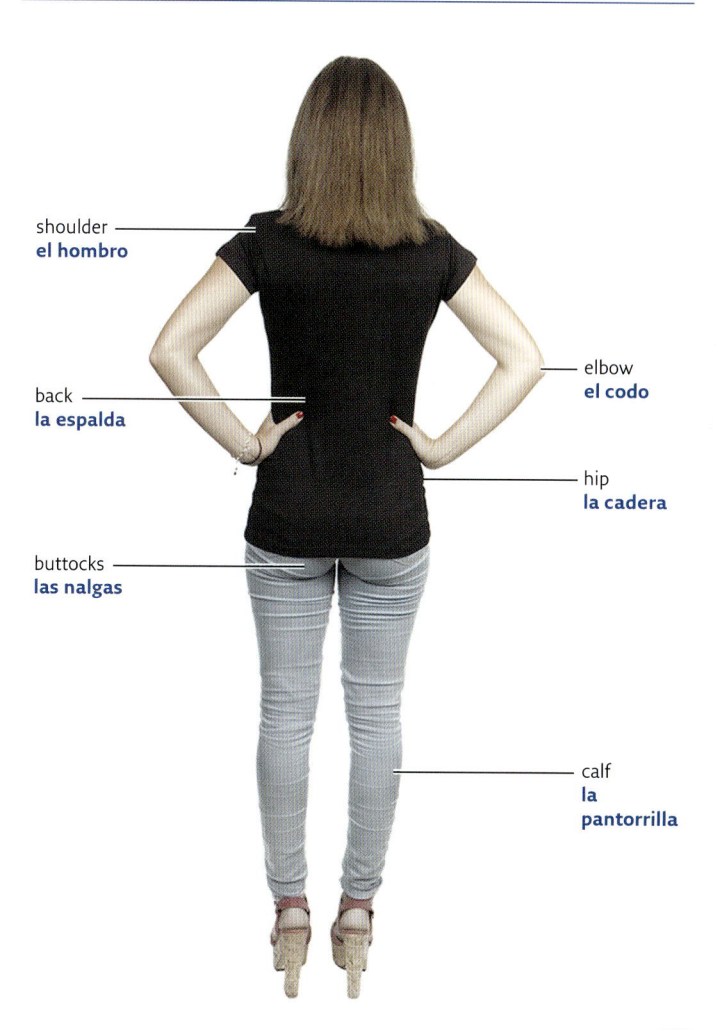

shoulder
el hombro

back
la espalda

buttocks
las nalgas

elbow
el codo

hip
la cadera

calf
la pantorrilla

THE SKELETON | EL ESQUELETO

Hopefully this is not vocabulary you will need very often, but it is useful to have the necessary terminology at your disposal should the need arise.

VOCABULARY

organ **el órgano**	intestines **los intestinos**	nerve **el nervio**
brain **el cerebro**	digestive system **el aparato digestivo**	tendon **el tendón**
heart **el corazón**	bladder **la vejiga**	tissue **el tejido**
lung **el pulmón**	blood **la sangre**	cell **la célula**
liver **el hígado**	joint **la articulación**	artery **la arteria**
stomach **el estómago**	bone **el hueso**	vein **la vena**
kidney **el riñón**	muscle **el músculo**	oxygen **el oxígeno**

YOU SHOULD KNOW...

As in English, parts of the body feature often in common Spanish expressions, such as:
"meter la pata" meaning "to make a blunder" (literally: to put your paw in it)
"tener dos dedos de frente" meaning "to have common sense" (literally: to have a forehead two fingers high)
"costar un riñón" meaning "to cost a fortune" (literally: to cost a kidney).

SKELETON

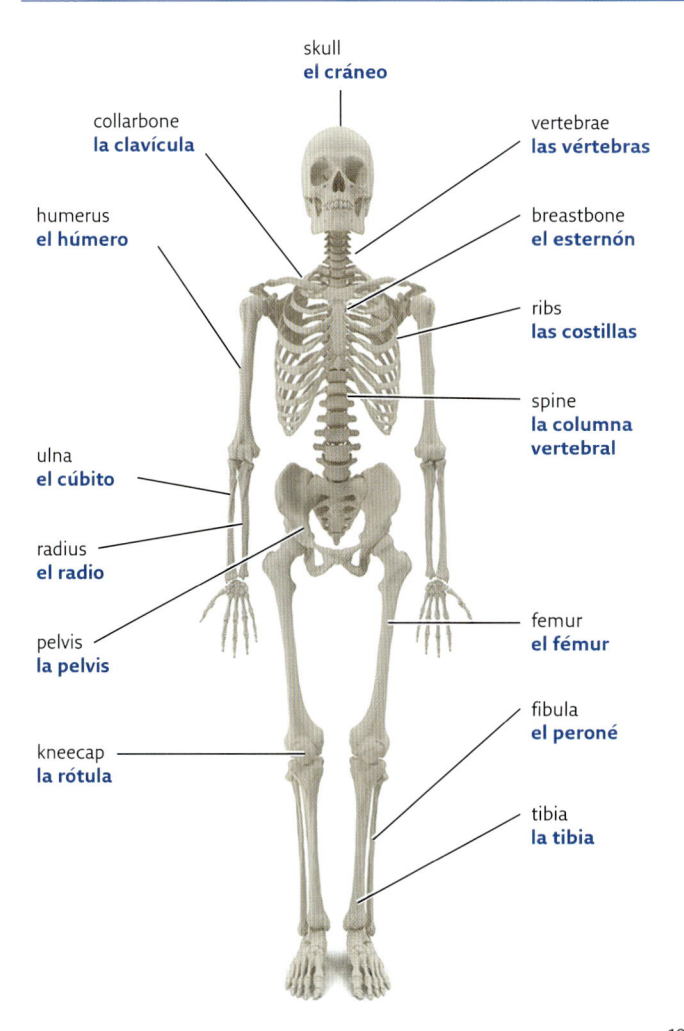

- skull **el cráneo**
- collarbone **la clavícula**
- vertebrae **las vértebras**
- humerus **el húmero**
- breastbone **el esternón**
- ribs **las costillas**
- spine **la columna vertebral**
- ulna **el cúbito**
- radius **el radio**
- pelvis **la pelvis**
- femur **el fémur**
- fibula **el peroné**
- kneecap **la rótula**
- tibia **la tibia**

THE DOCTOR'S SURGERY | LA CONSULTA

Spaniards can normally choose their "médico de familia" (family doctor or GP). Patients must be referred by their primary care doctor to any specialist, except in cases of emergency. When attending a doctor's appointment, you must bring your "Tarjeta Sanitaria"; if you don't have it to hand, you must present a form of ID.

YOU MIGHT SAY...

I'd like to make an appointment.
Quiero pedir una cita.

That hurts.
Duele.

I have an appointment with Dr...
Tengo una cita con el doctor...

I'm allergic to...
Soy alérgico a...

I take medication for...
Tomo medicamentos para...

I've been feeling unwell.
Últimamente no me he sentido bien.

YOU MIGHT HEAR...

Your appointment is at...
Su cita es a las...

The doctor will call you through.
El médico le llamará para que pase.

What are your symptoms?
¿Qué síntomas tiene?

May I examine you?
¿Puedo examinarle?

Tell me if that hurts.
Diga si le duele.

Do you have any allergies?
¿Tiene alguna alergia?

Do you take any medication?
¿Toma algún medicamento?

You need to see a specialist.
Necesita ver a un especialista.

VOCABULARY

appointment
la cita

clinic
el consultorio

specialist
el especialista / la especialista

examination
el examen médico

test
la prueba

prescription
la receta

medication
la medicación

sleeping pill
el somnífero

home visit
la visita a domicilio

antibiotics
los antibióticos

to examine
examinar

vaccination
la vacuna

the pill
la píldora (anticonceptiva)

to be on medication
tomar medicación

blood pressure monitor
el tensiómetro

examination room
la sala de reconocimiento

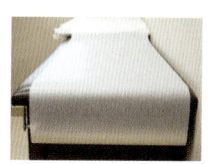

examination table
la mesa de exploración

GP
el médico de familia / la médica de familia

practice nurse
el auxiliar sanitario / la auxiliar sanitaria

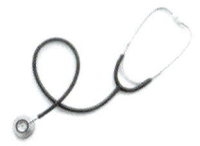

stethoscope
el estetoscopio

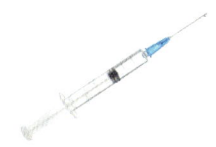

syringe
la jeringuilla

thermometer
el termómetro

waiting room
la sala de espera

THE DENTIST'S SURGERY | LA CONSULTA DEL DENTISTA

YOU MIGHT SAY...

I have toothache.
Me duele una muela.

I have an abscess.
Tengo un absceso dental.

My filling has come out.
Se me ha desprendido el empaste.

I've broken my tooth.
Se me ha roto un diente.

My dentures are broken.
Se me ha roto la dentadura postiza.

YOU MIGHT HEAR...

We don't have any emergency appointments available.
No nos quedan citas de emergencia.

You need a new filling.
Tenemos que ponerle otro empaste.

Your tooth has to come out.
Tenemos que quitarle un diente.

You have to make another appointment.
Tiene que pedir otra cita.

VOCABULARY

dental check-up **la revisión dental**	toothache **el dolor de muelas**	root canal treatment **la endodoncia**
molar **la muela**	abscess **el absceso**	extraction **la extracción**
incisor **el incisivo**	filling **el empaste**	to brush one's teeth **cepillarse los dientes**
wisdom teeth **las muelas del juicio**	crown **la corona**	to floss **usar el hilo dental**

YOU SHOULD KNOW...

Spanish has two different words for "tooth", depending on whether you are referring to a back tooth ("la muela"), or to one of the front teeth ("el diente").

braces
los brákets

dental floss
el hilo dental

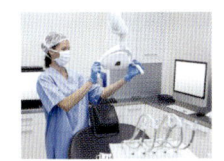

dental nurse
**el enfermero dental /
la enfermera dental**

dentist
**el dentista /
la dentista**

dentist's chair
la silla del dentista

dentist's drill
el torno del dentista

dentures
la dentadura postiza

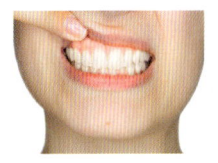

gums
las encías

mouthwash
el enjuague bucal

teeth
los dientes

toothbrush
el cepillo de dientes

toothpaste
el dentífrico

THE OPTICIAN'S | LA ÓPTICA

Eye tests in Spain are usually carried out by opticians, who can provide you with a prescription for glasses or contact lenses. Treatments for other kinds of eye conditions, including laser eye surgery, are usually carried out by ophthalmologists.

YOU MIGHT SAY...

I'd like to book an appointment.
Quiero pedir una cita.

My eyes are dry.
Tengo los ojos secos.

My eyes are sore.
Me duelen los ojos.

Do you repair glasses?
¿Arreglan gafas?

YOU MIGHT HEAR...

Your appointment is at...
Su cita es a las...

Look up/down/ahead.
Mire hacia arriba / hacia abajo / hacia adelante.

Read the letters on the first/second row.
Lea las letras de la primera / segunda línea.

VOCABULARY

ophthalmologist
el oftalmólogo / la oftalmóloga

reading glasses
las gafas de lectura

bifocals
las gafas bifocales

hard/soft contact lenses
las lentillas rígidas / blandas

lens
la lente

conjunctivitis
la conjuntivitis

stye
el orzuelo

blurred vision
la visión borrosa

cataracts
las cataratas

short-sighted
miope

long-sighted
hipermétrope

visually impaired
con discapacidad visual

blind
ciego

colour-blind
daltónico

to wear glasses
usar gafas

to wear contacts
usar lentillas

contact lenses
las lentillas

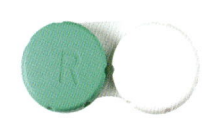

contact lens case
el estuche de las lentillas

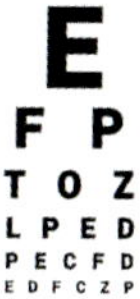

eye chart
la tabla optométrica

eye drops
el colirio

eye test
el examen ocular

frames
la montura

glasses
las gafas

glasses case
el estuche de gafas

optician
el oculista / la oculista

205

THE HOSPITAL | EL HOSPITAL

There are both public and private hospitals available in Spain. Many private hospitals do work for the state healthcare system, and social and private health insurance should cover most expenses, whether you visit a public or private facility.

YOU MIGHT SAY...

Which ward is ... in?
¿En qué sala está...?

When are visiting hours?
¿Cuál es el horario de visitas?

YOU MIGHT HEAR...

He/She is in ward...
Está en la sala...

Visiting hours are between ... and...
El horario de visitas va de las ... a las...

VOCABULARY

public/private hospital
el hospital público / privado

A&E
Urgencias

physiotherapist
el fisioterapeuta / la fisioterapeuta

radiographer
el radiógrafo / la radiógrafa

surgeon
el cirujano / la cirujana

ambulance
la ambulancia

operation
la operación quirúrgica

scan
el escáner

intensive care
los cuidados intensivos

defibrillator
el desfibrilador

diagnosis
el diagnóstico

pulse
el pulso

to take his/her pulse
tomar el pulso

to undergo surgery
someterse a una operación

to be admitted
ingresar en el hospital

to be discharged
recibir el alta

crutches
las muletas

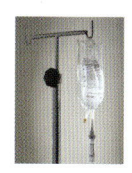

drip
el gotero

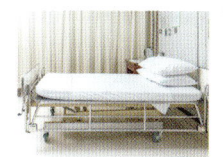

hospital bed
la cama de hospital

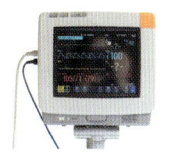

monitor
el monitor

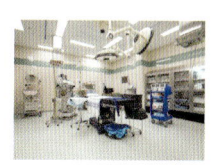

operating theatre
el quirófano

oxygen mask
la máscara de oxígeno

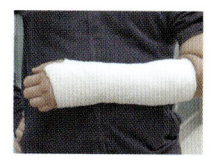

plaster cast
la escayola

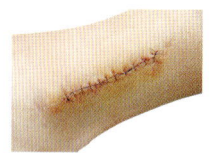

stitches
los puntos

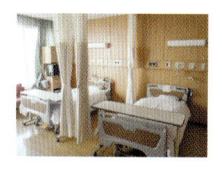

ward
la sala de hospital

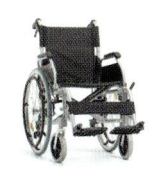

wheelchair
la silla de ruedas

X-ray
la radiografía

Zimmer frame®
el andador

INJURY | LAS LESIONES

YOU MIGHT SAY...

Can you help me?
¿Puede ayudarme?

I've had an accident.
He tenido un accidente.

I've hurt my...
Me he hecho daño en el / la...

I've broken/sprained my...
Me he roto / torcido el / la...

I've cut/burnt myself.
Me he cortado / quemado.

I've hit my head.
Me he dado un golpe en la cabeza.

YOU MIGHT HEAR...

Where does it hurt?
¿Dónde le duele?

Are you able to move it?
¿Puede moverlo?

Tell me what happened.
Cuénteme qué le pasó.

Do you feel faint?
¿Siente que se va a desmayar?

Do you feel sick?
¿Se siente mareado?

I'm calling an ambulance.
Voy a llamar a una ambulancia.

YOU SHOULD KNOW...

In Spain, if you phone for an ambulance, there will be an over-the-phone assessment to check what kind of service is required: some ambulances provide basic vital support, others offer advanced vital support (provided by a doctor), and some vehicles are used only for patient transportation.

VOCABULARY

accident
el accidente

concussion
la conmoción cerebral

fall
la caída

dislocation
la luxación

sprain
el esguince

scar
la cicatriz

whiplash
el latigazo

swelling
la hinchazón

recovery position
la postura de recuperación

CPR	**la reanimación cardiopulmonar**
to be unconscious	**estar sin sentido**
to injure oneself	**lesionarse**
to fall	**caerse**
to break one's arm	**romperse un brazo**
to twist one's ankle	**torcerse el tobillo**

INJURIES

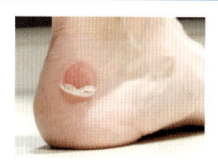

blister **la ampolla**	bruise **la magulladura**	burn **la quemadura**
cut **el corte**	fracture **la fractura**	graze **la rozadura**
splinter **la astilla**	sting **la picadura**	sunburn **la quemadura del sol**

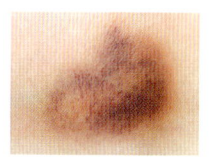

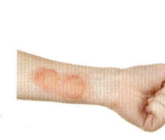

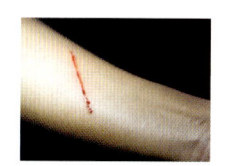

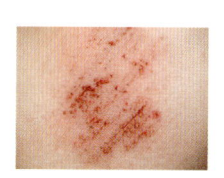

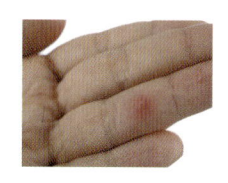

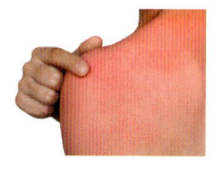

FIRST AID

antiseptic
el antiséptico

bandage
el vendaje

dressing
la gasa

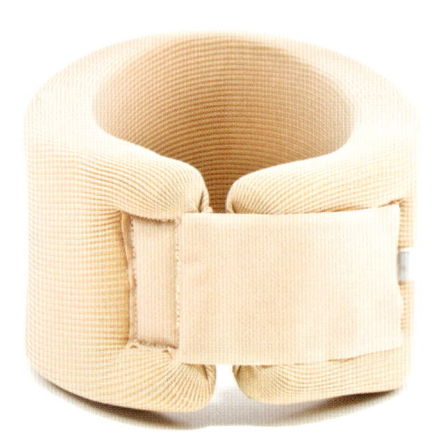

ice pack
la compresa de hielo

neck brace
el collarín cervical

ointment
la pomada

plaster
la tirita

sling
el cabestrillo

tweezers
las pinzas

ILLNESS | LA ENFERMEDAD

YOU MIGHT SAY...

I have a cold/the flu.
Tengo un resfriado / la gripe.

I have a sore stomach.
Me duele el estómago.

I'm going to be sick.
Voy a vomitar.

I'm asthmatic/diabetic.
Tengo asma. / Soy diabético.

YOU MIGHT HEAR...

You should go to the doctor.
Debería ir al médico.

You need to rest.
Tiene que descansar.

Do you need anything?
¿Necesita algo?

VOCABULARY

heart attack
el ataque cardíaco

stroke
el ictus

infection
la infección

ear infection
la infección de oído

virus
el virus

chicken pox
la varicela

rash
el sarpullido

stomach bug
el virus estomacal

vomiting
los vómitos

food poisoning
la intoxicación alimentaria

nausea
la náusea

diarrhoea
la diarrea

constipation
el estreñimiento

diabetes
la diabetes

epilepsy
la epilepsia

asthma
el asma *f*

inhaler
el inhalador

insulin
la insulina

period pain
los dolores menstruales

to have high/low blood pressure
tener la tensión alta / baja

to cough
toser

to sneeze
estornudar

to vomit
vomitar

to faint
desmayarse

PREGNANCY | EL EMBARAZO

If you plan to have your baby in Spain, you will be referred to a gynaecologist. He or she will be your principal contact during the pregnancy, give advice on maternity hospitals and midwives, and attend during the birth of the baby. If you are travelling while pregnant, make sure you have appropriate travel insurance in place.

YOU MIGHT SAY…

I'm (six months) pregnant.
Estoy embarazada (de seis meses).

My partner/wife is pregnant.
Mi pareja / mujer está embarazada.

I'm/She's having contractions every … minutes.
Tengo / Tiene contracciones cada … minutos.

My/Her waters have broken.
He / Ha roto aguas.

I need pain relief.
Necesito algo para el dolor.

YOU MIGHT HEAR…

How far along are you?
¿De cuántos meses está?

How long is it between contractions?
¿Cuánto tiempo pasa entre las contracciones?

May I examine you?
¿Puedo examinarle?

Push!
¡Empuje!

VOCABULARY

pregnant woman
la mujer embarazada

newborn
recién nacido

foetus
el feto

uterus
el útero

cervix
el cuello del útero

epidural
la epidural

gas and air
el gas de la risa

labour
el parto

Caesarean section
la cesárea

miscarriage
el aborto espontáneo

stillborn **mortinato**	to fall pregnant **quedarse embarazada**	to give birth **dar a luz**
due date **la fecha estimada de parto**	to go past one's due date **salir de cuentas**	to miscarry **tener un aborto (espontáneo)**
morning sickness **las náuseas del embarazo**	to be in labour **estar de parto**	to breast-feed **amamantar**

YOU SHOULD KNOW...

A full-term pregnancy in Spain is classed as 40 weeks and 6 days, as opposed to 39 weeks and 6 days in the UK. It is also common for parents to find out the baby's gender before birth, so let your health professionals know if you'd prefer a surprise!

incubator **la incubadora**	labour suite **la sala de parto**	midwife **la comadrona**
pregnancy test **el test de embarazo**	sonographer **el ecografista / la ecografista**	ultrasound **la ecografía**

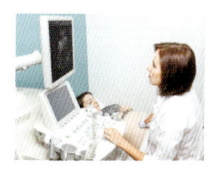

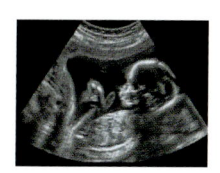

ALTERNATIVE THERAPIES | LAS TERAPIAS ALTERNATIVAS

Alternative therapies are becoming more popular in Spain, but not all are eligible for social security cover, so it is worth researching which treatments can be covered by standard insurance.

VOCABULARY

therapist
**el terapeuta /
la terapeuta**

chiropractor
**el quiropráctico /
la quiropráctica**

masseur
el masajista

masseuse
la masajista

acupuncturist
**el acupuntor /
la acupuntora**

reflexologist
**el reflexólogo /
la reflexóloga**

reiki
el reiki

mindfulness
la conciencia plena

to massage
dar un masaje a

to meditate
meditar

GENERAL

essential oil
el aceite esencial

herbal medicine
la fitoterapia

homeopathy
la homeopatía

THERAPIES

acupuncture
la acupuntura

chiropractic
la quiropráctica

hypnotherapy
la hipnoterapia

meditation
la meditación

reflexology
la reflexología

massage
el masaje

osteopathy
la osteopatía

thalassotherapy
la talasoterapia

traditional Chinese medicine
la medicina tradicional china

THE VET | EL VETERINARIO

If you intend to travel to Spain with your pet, they must be microchipped and vaccinated against rabies, and have a pet passport. Dogs must receive a tapeworm treatment from a vet 12-24 hours before returning to the UK.

YOU MIGHT SAY...

My dog/cat has been injured.
Mi perro / gato se ha lesionado.

My dog/cat has been sick.
Mi perro / gato ha devuelto.

YOU MIGHT HEAR...

What's the problem?
¿Cuál es el problema?

Is your pet microchipped?
¿Tiene su mascota un microchip?

YOU SHOULD KNOW...

Not all rental properties accept pets, so check before you book.

VOCABULARY

vet
el veterinario / la veterinaria

pet
la mascota

flea
la pulga

tick
la garrapata

rabies vaccination
la vacunación antirrábica

tapeworm treatment
el tratamiento antiparasitario

pet passport
el pasaporte para animales

quarantine
la cuarentena

to go to the vet
ir al veterinario

to spay/neuter
esterilizar / castrar

to put down
sacrificar

E-collar
el collarín

flea collar
el collar antiparasitario

pet carrier
el porta mascotas

PLANET EARTH | EL PLANETA TIERRA

Spain is full of diverse, wonderful landscapes: deserts, marshlands, spectacular mountains, and deep river valleys. Its varied climate – wet and cool in the north, dry and hot in the south – also provides a wide variety of habitats for wildlife. A large network of nature trails, as well numerous nature reserves and natural marine parks, give visitors plenty of opportunities to explore Spain's natural treasures for themselves.

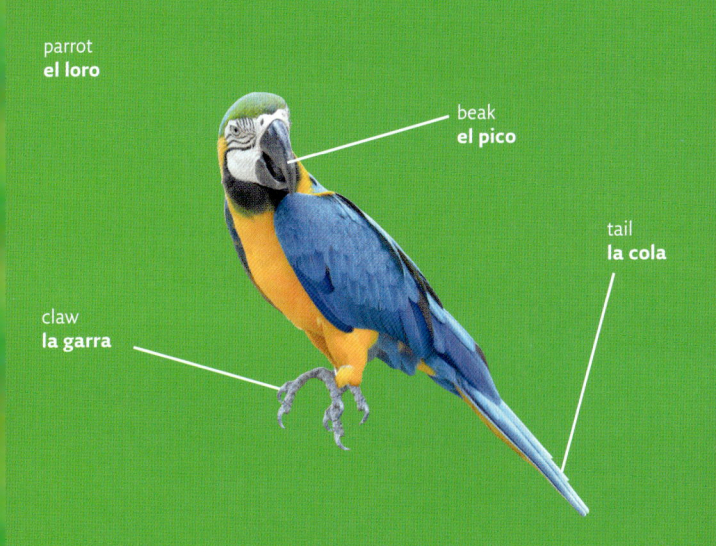

parrot
el loro

beak
el pico

tail
la cola

claw
la garra

THE BASICS | LO ESENCIAL

YOU MIGHT SAY...

Is there a park/nature reserve nearby?
¿Hay un parque / una reserva natural cerca?

What is the scenery like?
¿Cómo es el paisaje?

I enjoy being outdoors.
Me gusta estar al aire libre.

YOU MIGHT HEAR...

The scenery is beautiful/rugged.
El paisaje es muy bello / agreste.

This is a protected area.
Es una zona protegida.

I'd recommend visiting...
Le recomiendo visitar...

VOCABULARY

animal **el animal**	paw **la zarpa**	beak **el pico**
bird **el ave** *f*	hoof **la pezuña**	cold-blooded **de sangre fría**
fish **el pez**	snout **el morro**	warm-blooded **de sangre caliente**
species **la especie**	mane **la crin**	to bark **ladrar**
nature reserve **la reserva natural**	tail **la cola**	to purr **ronronear**
scenery **el paisaje**	claw **la garra**	to growl **gruñir**
zoo **el zoológico**	horn **el cuerno**	to roar **rugir**
fur **la piel**	feather **la pluma**	to chirp **piar**
wool **la lana**	wing **el ala** *f*	to buzz **zumbar**

218

DOMESTIC ANIMALS AND BIRDS
LOS ANIMALES DOMÉSTICOS

Almost 40% of Spanish households have a pet, and you will find plenty of veterinary facilities in the country. If you are planning to travel with your pet, check that the hotel or apartment you book is happy to have animals. Some public areas, like parks and beaches, may be off-limits for dogs.

YOU MIGHT SAY...

Do you have any pets?
¿Tienes mascotas?

Is it OK to bring my pet?
¿Puedo traer mi mascota?

This is my guide dog/assistance dog.
Este es mi perro guía / perro de asistencia.

My pet is missing.
Mi mascota se ha perdido.

YOU MIGHT HEAR...

I have/don't have a pet.
Tengo / No tengo una mascota.

I'm allergic to pet hair.
Soy alérgico al pelo de animales.

Animals are/are not allowed.
Los animales están / no están permitidos.

VOCABULARY

farmer
el agricultor / la agricultora

farm
la granja

owner
el dueño / la dueña

barn
el granero

meadow
el prado

hay
el heno

straw
la paja

guide dog
el perro guía

puppy
el cachorro

kitten
el gatito

lamb
el cordero

calf
el ternero

foal
el potro

fish food
la comida para peces

cat litter
la arena para gatos

to have a pet
tener una mascota

to walk the dog
sacar a pasear al perro

PETS

budgerigar
el periquito

canary
el canario

cat
el gato

dog
el perro

goldfish
el pececito rojo

guinea pig
la cobaya

hamster
el hámster

parrot
el loro

pony
el poni

rabbit
el conejo

rat
la rata

tropical fish
los peces tropicales

FARM ANIMALS

bull
el toro

chicken
el pollo

cow
la vaca

donkey
el burro

duck
el pato

goat
la cabra

goose
la oca

horse
el caballo

pig
el cerdo

sheep
la oveja

sheepdog
el perro pastor

turkey
el pavo

GENERAL

aquarium
el acuario

cage
la jaula

catflap
la gatera

collar
el collar

dog basket
la cesta del perro

hutch
la conejera

kennel
la caseta del perro

lead
la traílla

litter tray
la bandeja de la arena

muzzle
el bozal

pet food
la comida para mascotas

stable
la cuadra

AMPHIBIANS AND REPTILES | LOS ANFIBIOS Y REPTILES

alligator
el caimán

crocodile
el cocodrilo

frog
la rana

gecko
el geco

iguana
la iguana

lizard
el lagarto

newt
el tritón

salamander
la salamandra

snake
la serpiente

toad
el sapo

tortoise
la tortuga de tierra

turtle
la tortuga

MAMMALS | LOS MAMÍFEROS

badger
el tejón

bat
el murciélago

boar
el jabalí

deer
el ciervo

fox
el zorro

hare
la liebre

hedgehog
el erizo

mole
el topo

mouse
el ratón

otter
la nutria

squirrel
la ardilla

wolf
el lobo

OTHER COMMON MAMMALS

bear
el oso

camel
el camello

chimpanzee
el chimpancé

elephant
el elefante

giraffe
la jirafa

gorilla
el gorila

hippopotamus
el hipopótamo

kangaroo
el canguro

lion
el león

monkey
el mono

rhinoceros
el rinoceronte

tiger
el tigre

BIRDS | LAS AVES

blackbird
el mirlo

crane
la grulla

crow
el cuervo

dove
la paloma

eagle
el águila *f*

finch
el pinzón

flamingo
el flamenco

gull
la gaviota

hawk
el halcón

heron
la garza

kingfisher
el martín pescador

lark
la alondra

ostrich
el avestruz

owl
el búho

peacock
el pavo real

pelican
el pelícano

penguin
el pingüino

pigeon
la paloma

robin
el petirrojo

sparrow
el gorrión

stork
la cigüeña

swallow
la golondrina

swan
el cisne

vulture
el buitre

MINIBEASTS | LOS BICHOS PEQUEÑOS

VOCABULARY

swarm
el enjambre

cobweb
la telaraña

to buzz
zumbar

colony
la colonia

insect bite
la picadura de insecto

to sting
picar

ant
la hormiga

bee
la abeja

beetle
el escarabajo

butterfly
la mariposa

caterpillar
la oruga

centipede
el ciempiés

cockroach
la cucaracha

cricket
el grillo

dragonfly
la libélula

earthworm **la lombriz**	fly **la mosca**	grasshopper **el saltamontes**
ladybird **la mariquita**	mayfly **la cachipolla**	mosquito **el mosquito**
moth **la polilla**	slug **la babosa**	snail **el caracol**
spider **la araña**	wasp **la avispa**	woodlouse **la cochinilla**

MARINE CREATURES | LAS CRIATURAS MARINAS

coral
el coral

crab
el cangrejo

dolphin
el delfín

eel
la anguila

jellyfish
la medusa

killer whale
la orca

lobster
la langosta

seal
la foca

sea urchin
el erizo de mar

shark
el tiburón

starfish
la estrella de mar

whale
la ballena

FLOWERS, PLANTS, AND TREES
LAS FLORES, LAS PLANTAS Y LOS ÁRBOLES

VOCABULARY

stalk **el tallo**	bud **el brote**	branch **la rama**
leaf **la hoja**	seed **la semilla**	trunk **el tronco**
petal **el pétalo**	bulb **el bulbo**	bark **la corteza**
pollen **el polen**	wood **el bosque**	root **la raíz**

YOU SHOULD KNOW...

In Spain, chrysanthemums are used as cemetery flowers, white flowers are traditionally for bridal bouquets, and the poinsettia is associated with Christmas.

FLOWERS

bougainvillea
la buganvilla

carnation
el clavel

chrysanthemum
el crisantemo

daffodil
el narciso

daisy
la margarita

geranium
el geranio

hyacinth
el jacinto

iris
el iris

lily
la azucena

orchid
la orquídea

pansy
el pensamiento

poinsettia
la flor de pascua

poppy
la amapola

rose
la rosa

sunflower
el girasol

PLANTS AND TREES

almond tree
el almendro

chestnut
el castaño

cypress
el ciprés

fir
el abeto

fungus
el hongo

grapevine
la parra

ivy
la hiedra

laurel
el laurel

moss
el musgo

oak
el roble

olive
el olivo

pine
el pino

plane
el plátano

poplar
el álamo

willow
el sauce

LAND, SEA, AND SKY | LA TIERRA, EL MAR Y EL CIELO

VOCABULARY

landscape	estuary	rural
el paisaje	**el estuario**	**rural**
soil	air	urban
la tierra	**el aire**	**urbano**
mud	atmosphere	polar
el barro	**la atmósfera**	**polar**
water	sunrise	alpine
el agua *f*	**la salida del sol**	**alpino**
plateau	sunset	tropical
la meseta	**la puesta del sol**	**tropical**

LAND

cave
la cueva

desert
el desierto

farmland
la tierra de cultivo

forest
el bosque

glacier
el glaciar

grassland
el pastizal

hill
la colina

lake
el lago

marsh
la marisma

mountain
la montaña

pond
el estanque

river
el río

rocks
las rocas

scrub
el monte bajo

stream
el arroyo

valley
el valle

volcano
el volcán

waterfall
la cascada

SEA

cliff
el acantilado

coast
la costa

coral reef
el arrecife de coral

island
la isla

peninsula
la península

rockpool
la poza de marea

SKY

aurora
la aurora

clouds
las nubes

moon
la luna

rainbow
el arco iris

stars
las estrellas

sun
el sol

CELEBRATIONS AND FESTIVALS
LAS CELEBRACIONES Y LAS FIESTAS

"¡Estamos de fiesta!" Everyone loves having a reason to celebrate, and Spaniards need little excuse to get together and have a good time with friends or family over some good food and drink. In addition to the usual well-known holidays, there is also a wealth of Spanish customs and traditions associated with the various holidays and festivals throughout the year.

costume
el disfraz

feather
la pluma

mask
la máscara

THE BASICS | LO ESENCIAL

YOU MIGHT SAY/HEAR...

Congratulations!
¡Enhorabuena!

Well done!
¡Bien hecho!

Cheers!
¡Salud!

Happy birthday!
**¡Feliz cumpleaños! /
¡Felicidades!**

Happy anniversary!
¡Feliz aniversario!

Best wishes.
Mis mejores deseos.

And to you, too!
¡Igualmente!

You're very kind.
Eres muy amable.

Cheers to you, too!
¡A tu salud también!

VOCABULARY

occasion
la ocasión

public holiday
el día festivo

religious holiday
la fiesta religiosa

celebration
la celebración

surprise party
la fiesta sorpresa

birthday
el cumpleaños

birthday party
la fiesta de cumpleaños

wedding
la boda

wedding anniversary
el aniversario de bodas

good news
las buenas noticias

bad news
las malas noticias

to celebrate
celebrar

to throw a party
organizar una fiesta

to toast
brindar por

YOU SHOULD KNOW...

In Spain, as well as celebrating a person's birthday, it is also common to celebrate a person's name day ("el santo") – the feast day for the saint whose name a person shares.

bouquet
el ramo de flores

box of chocolates
la caja de bombones

bunting
las banderitas de colores

cake
la tarta

champagne
el champán

confetti
el confeti

decorations
las decoraciones

funfair
la feria

gift
el regalo

greetings card
la tarjeta de felicitación

party
la fiesta

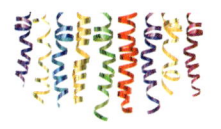

streamers
las serpentinas

HIGH DAYS AND HOLIDAYS | LAS FIESTAS

There are 12 national public holidays per year plus 2 local ones. While these don't automatically shift if they fall on a weekend, it is commonplace to take an additional Friday or Monday off if the holiday falls on Thursday or Tuesday in order to "hacer puente" (literally "to make the bridge").

YOU MIGHT SAY/HEAR...

Is it a holiday today?
¿Es fiesta hoy?

I wish you...
Te deseo...

What are your plans for the holiday?
¿Qué planes tienes para las vacaciones?

Happy Easter!
¡Que pases una buena Semana Santa!

Eid Mubarak!
¡Eid Mubarak!

Happy holidays!
¡Felices vacaciones!

VOCABULARY

birth
el nacimiento

baby shower
la fiesta de nacimiento

christening
el bautizo

First Communion
la primera comunión

bar mitzvah
el bar mitzvah

bat mitzvah
el bat mitzvah

finding a job
encontrar un trabajo

graduation
la graduación

engagement
el compromiso (matrimonial)

marriage
el matrimonio

divorce
el divorcio

relocation
el traslado

retirement
la jubilación

funeral
el funeral

Mother's Day
el Día de la Madre

Father's Day
el Día del Padre

Valentine's Day
el Día de los Enamorados

Halloween
Halloween

GENERAL

All Saints' Day
el Día de Todos los Santos

Chinese New Year
el Año Nuevo chino

Diwali
Diwali

Easter
la Semana Santa

Eid-al-Fitr
Eid-al-Fitr

Hanukkah
Janucá

Holi
Holi

Passover
la Pascua

Ramadan
el Ramadán

SPANISH FESTIVALS

Buñol Tomatina
la Tomatina de Buñol

Fallas festivities
las Fallas

Running of the Bulls
los sanfermines

CHRISTMAS AND NEW YEAR
LA NAVIDAD Y EL AÑO NUEVO

Christmas is usually celebrated on December 24th ("la Nochebuena", literally "the Good Night") and 25th in Spain – families will gather to have dinner on Christmas Eve, and some will attend midnight mass ("la misa del gallo", literally "the cockerel's mass"). Traditionally, presents are exchanged on Epiphany (January 6th) rather than Christmas Day. On December 28th (Holy Innocents' Day, or "el día de los Santos Inocentes"), it is customary to play practical jokes on people, similar to the way April Fools' Day is celebrated in the UK.

YOU MIGHT SAY/HEAR...

Merry Christmas!
¡Feliz Navidad!

Fooled you!
¡Inocente!

Happy New Year!
¡Feliz Año Nuevo!

VOCABULARY

Christmas Eve **la Nochebuena**	Christmas tree **el árbol de Navidad**	New Year's Eve **la Nochevieja**
Christmas Day **el Día de Navidad**	Epiphany **el Día de Reyes**	New Year's Day **el Día De Año Nuevo**
Christmas card **la tarjeta de Navidad**		

YOU SHOULD KNOW...

On the morning of Epiphany, or the "Día de Reyes", it is traditional to eat "el Roscón de Reyes", a round cake decorated with candied fruits and baked with a charm ("la sorpresa") and sometimes a bean ("el haba") inside. The person who finds the charm in their portion is crowned with the cardboard crown, whereas it would be customary for the person who finds the bean to pay for the cake.

bauble
la bola

Christmas dinner
la comida de Navidad

Christmas lights
las luces navideñas

Christmas market
el mercadillo navideño

Father Christmas/Santa Claus
Papá Noel / Santa Claus

fireworks
los fuegos artificiales

king's cake
el Roscón de Reyes

Nativity scene
el Belén

the Three Kings
los Reyes Magos

YOU SHOULD KNOW...

The beginning of a new year is often marked with the tradition of eating the "lucky grapes" ("las uvas de la suerte"). The custom is for people to eat 12 grapes, one for every chime of the clock at 12 a.m. on January 1st. Those who successfully manage this challenge are guaranteed good fortune for the coming year.

CARNIVAL | EL CARNAVAL

There is a strong tradition of Carnival celebrations in Spain, dating back to medieval times. It takes place just before the start of the "Cuaresma" (Lent) and is commonly celebrated in towns across Spain with colourful parades and music. Some Spanish Carnival celebrations, such as the ones in Tenerife or Cádiz, are famous internationally for their grand parades with floats and music. Many Carnival celebrations elsewhere in Spain are less formal, with groups of friends just dressing up as historical characters or in funny, sometimes surreal, outfits.

carnival float
la carroza de carnaval

costume
el disfraz

effigy
la figura de carnaval

face paint
la pintura facial

headdress
el tocado

mask
la máscara

parade
el desfile

street performer
el artista callejero / la artista callejera

INDEX | EL ÍNDICE

ENGLISH

ABOUT YOU 9
accessible parking space 25
accessories 103
accordion 158
acoustic guitar 158
acupuncture 214
aerial 50
aeroplane 40
airbag 29
air bed 153
air conditioning 49
airport 40
AIR TRAVEL 39
alligator 223
All Saints' Day 241
almond cake 121
almond tree 232
ALTERNATIVE THERAPIES 214
aluminium foil 54
American football 189
AMPHIBIANS AND REPTILES 223
anchor 43
ankle 195
ant 228
antifreeze 29
antiperspirant 95
antique shop 111
antiseptic 94, 210
apartment block 47
apple 80
apricot 80
aquarium 222
archery 189
arm 196
armbands 179
armchair 53, 61
art gallery 145
ARTS AND CRAFTS 164
artichoke 82
asparagus 82
assistant referee 173
athlete 186
ATHLETICS 186
ATM 136
aubergine 82
aurora 236
awning 64
baby bath 99
baby food 98
BABY GOODS 97
babygro® 97
baby lotion 98

baby's bottle 98
baby seat 99
baby sling 99
baby walker 99
back 197
backing group 160
bacon 87
badger 224
badminton 176
badminton racket 176
baggage reclaim 40
baguette 84, 115
baking tray 55
balcony 45
ball boy 177
ballet 147
ball girl 177
ball of wool 166
banana 69, 80
bandage 94, 191, 210
BANK 135
banknotes 72, 136
bar 123, 147
barber's 111
baseball cap 107
baseball game 189
BASICS 8, 18, 46, 70, 114, 142, 168, 192, 218, 238
basket 69, 74, 78, 175
BASKETBALL 175
basketball 175
basketball court 175
basketball game 175
basketball player 175
basketball shoes 175
bass drum 158
bass guitar 158
bat 224
bath 63
bath mat 62
BATHROOM 62
bathroom 63
bath towel 62
bauble 243
BEACH 154
beach ball 155
beach tent 155
beach towel 155
beak 217
bear 225
beauty salon 111

bed 61
BEDROOM 60
bedroom 61
bedside lamp 61
bedside table 61
bee 228
beer 76
beetle 228
beetroot 82
bell 33
belt 107
bib 97
BICYCLE 32
bicycle 33
bidet 63
big toe 195
bike lock 33
bikini 105, 155
bill 123
birdbox 66
BIRDS 226
biscuits 74
black 7
blackberry 80
blackbird 226
blade 17
blanket 60
blister 209
block of flats 45
blood pressure monitor 201
blouse 105
blue 7
blueberry 80
Bluetooth® speaker 158
Blu-ray® player 52
blusher 96
boar 224
board game 163
boarding card 41
BODY 194
body 196, 197
bodyboarding 179
boiler 49
bonnet 22
bookcase 52
bookshop 111
boot 22
bootees 97
boots 34, 108
bougainvillea 231
bouquet 239
boutique 111
bowl 59
bowling 163

box 138
boxer shorts 105
boxing gloves 184
boxing ring 184
boxing shoes 184
box of chocolates 239
bra 105
bracelet 107
braces 203
brake 33
bread 69
bread and tomatoes 115
bread basket 123
bread bin 54
bread rolls 84, 115
BREAKFAST 115
breastbone 199
brie 92
bridge 25
broccoli 82
broth 118
bruise 209
brush 67
Brussels sprout 82
bucket 67
bucket and spade 155
budgerigar 220
bull 221
bumper 22
Buñol Tomatina 241
buns 115
bunting 239
buoy 43
bureau de change 136
burger 87, 126
burn 209
BUS 30
bus 31
bus shelter 31
bus stop 31
BUTCHER'S 86
butter 91
butter-bean stew 118
butterfly 228
buttocks 197
buttons 166
cabbage 82
cabin 41
cabinet 63
cabrales 92
café 139
cafeteria 131

cage 222
cake 239
calamari 120
calculator 133
calf 197
camel 225
camera 145
camera lens 161
CAMPING 152
camping stove 153
campus 131
canary 220
canoe 44
canoeing 179
canvas 165
capsule 94
CAR 20
car 22
caravan 153
cardigan 105
card reader 72
cards 163
carnation 231
carnival 244
carnival 147
carnival float 244
carom billiards 189
car park 25
carriage 37
carrot 82
car showroom 111
car wash 25
casino 147
casserole dish 55
castle 145
cat 220
caterpillar 228
catflap 222
cathedral 139, 145
cauliflower 82
cave 234
ceiling fan 49
celery 82
cello 158
centipede 228
centre circle 167
cereal 115
chain 33
chair 123
champagne 239
champagne flute 59, 123
changing bag 98
changing room 170
charger 128

245

charity shop 111
check-in desk 41
cheddar 92
cheek 195
CHEESE AND DAIRY PRODUCTS 91
cheesecake 121
cheese knife 123
cherry 80
chess 163
chest 196
chestnut tree 232
chest of drawers 61
chicken 221
chicken breast 87
chickpea stew 119
chilli 82
chimney 50
chimpanzee 225
chin 195
Chinese New Year 241
chiropractic 214
chisel 109
chocolate 76
chocolate cake 121
chocolate mousse 121
choir 160
chop 87
chopping board 55
chorizo 87
CHRISTMAS AND NEW YEAR 242
Christmas dinner 243
Christmas lights 243
Christmas market 243
chrysanthemum 231
church 139
churros 84
churros and chocolate 116, 126
cigar 100
cigarette 100
cinema 147
circus 147
city map 145
clam 90
clarinet 158
claw 217
cliff 236
climbing 189
clingfilm 54
clock radio 60
cloth 67
clothes horse 67
clothes pegs 67
CLOTHING AND FOOTWEAR 104
clouds 236
coach 31

coast 236
coat 105
coat hanger 60
cockle 90
cockpit 17, 41
cockroach 228
cod 89
coffee 116
coffee pot 55
coffee table 53
coffee with milk 113, 116
coins 72
colander 55
cold meats 118
collar 222
collarbone 199
colouring pencils 130
comb 95
COMBAT SPORTS 184
comedy show 148
comic book 100
COMMUNICATION AND IT 127
compact camera 161
computer 128
concert 148
conditioner 95
condom 94
conductor 160
conference centre 139
confetti 239
confectionery 100
contact lens case 205
contact lenses 205
cooking 143
cool box 153
coral 230
coral reef 236
corkscrew 55
corridor 150
cosmetics 103
costume 237, 244
cot 99
cotton bud 98
cotton wool 98
couchette 37
cough mixture 94
counters 163
courgette 82
courthouse 139
couscous 74, 118
cow 221
crab 90, 230
crampons 182
crane 226
crate 78
crayfish 90
cream 91
credit card 72
crème brûlée 121

crème caramel 121
cricket 228
crisps 76
crochet hook 166
crocodile 223
croissant 85, 116
croquettes 120
crossbar 33
cross trainer 170
crossword 163
crow 226
crutches 207
cucumber 83
cup 113
cup and saucer 59
cupboard 57
curtains 52, 61
cushion 53
custard pudding 121
customers 78
cut 209
cymbals 159
cypress 232
daffodil 231
daisy 231
Danish pastry 85
darts 163
dashboard 23
DAYS, MONTHS, A ND SEASONS 15
debit card 136
deckchair 155
decking 64
decorations 239
deep-fat fryer 55
deer 224
dental floss 203
dental nurse 203
dentist 203
dentist's chair 203
dentist's drill 203
DENTIST'S SURGERY 202
dentures 203
DEPARTMENT STORE 102
departure board 37, 41
desert 234
desk 133
desk lamp 133
detached house 47
dice 163
DINING ROOM 58
discus 186
dishwasher 67
display cabinet 52
diving board 179
Diwali 241
DIY 143
DIY STORE 109
DJ 160

"do not disturb" sign 150
doctor 193
DOCTOR'S SURGERY 200
dog 220
dog basket 222
dolphin 230
DOMESTIC ANIMALS AND BIRDS 219
dominoes 163
donkey 221
door 22
doorbell 51
double bass 159
double room 150
doughnut 85
dove 226
dragonfly 228
draining board 55
drainpipe 50
draughts 163
drawer 57
dress 106
dressing 210
dressing gown 106
dressing table 60
drip 207
DRIVING 24
driveway 50
drone 161
drops 94
DSLR camera 161
duck 221
dumbbells 170
dummy 99
dungarees 106
dustbin 68
dustpan 68
duty-free shop 41
duvet 61
DVD player 52
eagle 226
ear 195
earphones 158
earrings 108
earthworm 229
easel 165
Easter 241
EATING OUT 122
e-cigarette 100
éclair 85
E-collar 216
EDUCATION 129
eel 230
effigy 244
egg 91
Eid-al-Fitr 241
elbow 197
electrical store 111
electric drill 109
electric guitar 159
elephant 225

embroidery 164
emergency phone 29
Emmenthal 92
ENTRANCE 51
envelope 100, 138
eraser 130
essential oil 214
estate agency 111
EVENINGS OUT 146
examination room 201
examination table 201
exchange rate 136
exercise bike 171
exercise book 130
extension cable 49
eye 195
eye chart 205
eye drops 205
eyeliner 96
eyeshadow 96
eye test 205
fabada 119
fabric 166
fabric scissors 166
face 195, 196
face paint 244
Fallas festivities 241
FAMILY AND FRIENDS 10
farmhouse 47
farmland 234
fashion 103
FAST FOOD 125
Father Christmas 243
feather 237
femur 199
fence 66
fencing 185
ferry 44
FERRY AND BOAT TRAVEL 42
fibula 199
filing cabinet 133
filled baguette 126
fillet 87
finch 226
finger 195
fingernail 195
fir 233
fireplace 53
fire station 139
fireworks 243
first aid 211
first-aid kit 191, 193
fishing 189
fish knife 124
FISHMONGER'S 83
fizzy drink 76
flamingo 226
flea collar 216

246

flip-flops 155	garden hose 64	hairdresser's 112	hotel 140	keyboard 159
flippers 156, 179	gardening 143	hairdryer 60	HOUSE 48	key card 151
florist's 111	gardening gloves 64	hairspray 96	house 50	kickboxing 185
flowerpot 66	gardens 145	hake 89	HOUSEWORK 67	killer whale 230
flowers 66	garden shed 64	hake with salsa verde	humerus 199	kingfisher 226
FLOWERS, PLANTS,	garlic 83	119	hurdles 186	king's cake 243
AND TREES 231	gate 50, 66	ham 87	hutch 222	KITCHEN 54
flute 159	gazpacho 119	hammer 109	hyacinth 232	kitchen 57
fly 229	gears 33	hamster 220	hypnotherapy 214	kitchen knife 56
flysheet 141	gearstick 23	hand 195, 196	ice axe 182	kitchen roll 54
folder 133	gecko 223	handbag 168	ice cream 121	kitchenware 103
food and drink 103	GENERAL HEALTH 11	handball 189	ice hockey 189	kiwi fruit 80
food processor 55	geranium 231	hand blender 55	ice pack 210	knee 196
foot 195, 196	gift 239	handbrake 23	ice skates 182	kneecap 199
FOOTBALL 172	gift shop 112	handle 113	ice skating 182	knife and fork 59
football 173	giraffe 225	handlebars 33	icing sugar 74	knitting needles 166
football boots 173	glacier 234	hand mixer 55	ignition 23	knuckle 195
football match 173	glasses 205	hand towel 62	iguana 223	kung fu 185
football pitch 167,	glasses case 205	Hanukkah 241	ILLNESS 211	labour suite 213
173	glove compartment	harbour 43	incubator 213	lace-up shoes 108
football player 173	23	hare 224	indicator 22	ladle 56
footpump 153	gloves 108	harp 159	inflatable dinghy 44	ladybird 229
footstool 53	goal 167, 173	hawk 226	INJURY 208	lake 235
footwear 103	goalkeeper 173	head 196	ink 165	lamb chops 119
forehead 195	goalkeeper's gloves	headdress 244	insect repellent 94	LAND, SEA, AND SKY
forest 234	173	headguard 184	instant coffee 74	234
formula milk 98	goat 221	headlight 22	intercom 51	lane 25
foundation 96	goat's cheese 92	headphones 158	IN TOWN 139	laptop 133
fountain 140	goggles 179	headrest 23	iris 232	lark 226
fox 224	goldfish 220	health food shop 112	iron 68	laundrette 140
fracture 209	GOLF 188	helicopter 37	ironing board 68	laundry basket 60
frame 33	golf bag 188	helmet 33, 34	island 236	laurel 233
frames 205	golf ball 188	helmet cam 34	ivy 233	lawn 66
fridge-freezer 57	golf buggy 188	herbal medicine 214	jack 29	lawnmower 65
fried custard slice 121	golf club 188	herbs 74	jacket 106	lead 222
fried fish 119	goose 221	heron 226	jam 74, 116	leather gloves 34
fries 126	gorilla 225	herring 89	javelin 186	leather goods 103
frog 223	GP 201	hedgehog 224	jaw 195	leather jacket 34
front door 50	grape 80	heel 195	jeans 106	lecture hall 131
front light 33	grapefruit 80	helmet 33, 34	jellyfish 230	lecturer 131
FRUIT AND	grapevine 233	HIGH DAYS AND	jet ski 179	leek 83
VEGETABLES 79	grasshopper 229	HOLIDAYS 240	jetty 43	leg 196
fruit bowl 54	grassland 234	high heels 108	jeweller's 112	leggings 106
fruit juice 76	grater 55	high jump 186	jewellery-making 164	leisure centre 169
fruit tart 85	gravy boat 58	hill 235	jigsaw puzzle 163	lemon 80
frying pan 55	graze 209	hip 197	jogging 143	lentils 74
fuel gauge 23	green 7	hippopotamus 225	jogging bottoms 106	lentil stew 118
fuel pump 25	green beans 83	hi-viz vest 29	joint 87	letter 138
funfair 148, 239	greetings card 101,	hob 57	judo 185	letterbox 51
fungus 233	239	hockey 189	jug of water 124	lettuce 83
furniture 103	groundsheet 141	hoe 65	jumper 106	level crossing 25
furniture store 111	guard 37	holdall 41	jump leads 29	library 131, 140
fusebox 49	guidebook 145	hole punch 133	junction 25	lifebuoy 43
gable 50	guinea pig 220	Holi 241	kangaroo 225	lifeguard 179
Galician octopus 120	gull 226	homeopathy 214	karate 185	lifejacket 44, 180
GAMES 162	gums 203	honey 74	kayak 44	light bulb 49, 109
gaming 143	gutter 50	horse 221	kayaking 180	lighting 103
gangway 43	guy rope 141	horse racing 189	kebab 126	light railway 37
garage 29, 50	gym ball 171	HOSPITAL 206	kennel 222	lily 232
GARDEN 64	gymnastics 189	hospital 140, 193	kerb 25	line judge 177
garden 66	hacksaw 109	hospital bed 207	ketchup 74	liner 44
garden centre 111	hair 195	hot dog 126	kettle bell 171	lingerie 103
garden fork 64	hairbrush 96	HOTEL 149		lion 225

247

lip balm 96
lipstick 96
listening to music 143
litter tray 222
lizard 223
lobster 90, 230
locker 171
long jump 186
LOUNGE 52
lounge 53
lozenge 94
ludo 163
luggage rack 37
luggage trolley 41

mackerel 89
magazine 101
mahon 92
MAIN MEALS 117
MAMMALS 224
manchego 92
mango 80
map 91, 101
margarine 91
MARINE CREATURES 230
MARKET 77
marketplace 78
marmalade 75
marsh 235
mascara 96
mask 237, 244
massage 215
mat 153
matches 153
mattress 61
mayfly 229
mayonnaise 75
measuring jug 56
mechanic 29
medal 169
medicine 94, 193
meditation 215
melon 80
menu 124
meringue 121
meter 50
metro 37
microwave 57
midwife 213
milk 91
mille-feuille 85
mince 87
minibar 151
MINIBEASTS 228
minibus 28
mirror 61, 63
mittens 97
mixing bowl 56
mobile 99
model-making 164
mole 224
monitor 207

monkey 225
monkfish 89
monument 145
moon 236
mooring 44
mop 68
Moses basket 99
mosque 140
mosquito 229
moss 233
moth 229
MOTORBIKE 34
motorbike 34
motorcycle racing 189
motorhome 153
motor racing 190
motorway 25
mountain 235
mouse 224
mouth 195
mouthguard 184
mouth organ 159
mouthwash 95, 203
mozzarella 92
muesli 116
muffin 85, 116
museum 145
mushroom 83
MUSIC 157
musical 148
musician 160
music shop 112
music stand 160
mussel 90
mussels 120
muzzle 222

nail varnish 96
nails 109
napkin 58, 124
nappy 98
nappy cream 98
Nativity scene 243
neck 196
neck brace 210
necklace 108
needle and thread 166
netball 190
net curtains 61
newspaper 101
newt 223
nightclub 148
noodles 118, 126
nose 17, 195
notebook 101
notepad 133
number plate 22
nurse 193
nuts 76
nuts and bolts 109

oak 233
oars 180

octopus 90
OFFICE 132
office block 140
official 169
oil paint 165
ointment 210
olive 233
olive oil 75
olives 76, 120
omelette 126
onion 83
opera 148
operating theatre 207
optician 205
OPTICIAN'S 204
optician's 112
orange 81
orange juice 116
orchestra 160
orchid 232
ornament 53
osteopathy 215
ostrich 227
OTHER SHOPS 111
OTHER SPORTS 189
otter 224
oven 57
owl 227
oxygen mask 207
oyster 90

package 138
padded envelope 138
paddle 180
paddleboarding 180
paella 120
paella pan 56
paint 109
paintbrush 109, 165
paint roller 110
palette 165
palm 195
pancakes 117
pansy 232
pants 106
papaya 81
paper 130, 165
paper bag 72
paper clip 134
papercrafts 164
parade 244
paramedic 193
parking meter 25
parking space 25
parmesan 92
parrot 217, 220
parsol 65, 155
park 140
party 239
passion fruit 81
Passover 241
passport 41
pasta 75, 118

pastels 165
pasty 85
path 66
patient 193
patio 66
patio furniture 66
pavement 26
peach 81
peacock 227
pear 81
peas 83
pedal 33
pedal bin 54
peeler 56
pelican 227
pelvis 199
pen 101, 130, 165
penalty box 167
pencil 101, 130, 165
pencil case 131
penguin 227
peninsula 236
pepper 75
pepper mill 58
petanque 190
pet carrier 216
pet food 222
pet shop 112
petrol station 26
pharmacist 193
PHARMACY 193
pharmacy 193
phone shop 112
photocopier 134
PHOTOGRAPHY 161
piano 159
picture 53
pig 221
pigeon 227
pill 94
pillow 61
pilot 41
pine 233
pineapple 81
pins 166
piste 183
pizza 126
plane 233
plant pot 65
plaster 94, 191, 210
plaster cast 207
plastic bag 72, 78
plate 59
platform 37
playground 140
pliers 110
plum 81
podium 169
poinsettia 232
pole vault 187
police station 140
pomegranate 81
pond 235

pony 220
popcorn 76
poplar 233
poppy 232
port 44
porter 151
postal worker 138
postbox 138
postcard 101, 138
POST OFFICE 137
potato 83
potatoes 118
potatoes in spicy tomato sauce 120
potato salad 118
pothole 25
pottery 164
powder 96
practice nurse 201
pram 99
prawn 90
prawns in garlic sauce 120
PREGNANCY 212
pregnancy test 213
pressure cooker 56
printer 134
produce 78
promenade 156
pruners 65
pump 33
punchbag 184
pushchair 99
putter 188
puzzle book 101
pyjamas 106

quilt 61

rabbit 220
RACKET SPORTS 176
radiator 50
radio 21
radius 199
RAIL TRAVEL 35
rainbow 236
Ramadan 241
raspberry 81
rat 220
ratatouille 119
razor 95
reading 143
rearview mirror 23
receipt 72
reception 151
receptionist 151
red 7
red card 173
redcurrant 81
red pepper 83
referee 169
reflector 33
reflexology 215
refreshments trolley 37

248

relay 187
remote control 52
restaurant 148
restaurant car 38
reusable shopping bag 72
rhinoceros 225
ribs 87, 199
rice 75, 118
rice pudding 121
ricotta 92
ring binder 134
river 235
road 26
roast chicken 118
roast lamb 119
robin 227
rockpool 236
rocks 235
rolling pin 56
roof 22, 45, 50
rope 182
rose 232
rotor 17
round loaf 85
roundabout 26
rowing boat 44
rowing machine 171
rubber gloves 68
rubber ring 156
rucksack 153
rug 53, 61
RUGBY 174
rugby 174
rugby ball 174
rugby field 174
rugby goalposts 174
rugby player 174
ruler 131
Running of the Bulls 241
running track 187
runway 41
saddle 33
safe 151
safety deposit box 136
safety pin 166
sailing boat 44
salad 119
salad bowl 58
salamander 223
salmon 89
salopettes 183
salt 75
salt and pepper 124
salt cellar 58
sand 155
sandals 108
sandcastle 156
sandwich 126
sanitary towel 95
Santa Claus 243

sardine 89
sat nav 23
saucepan 56
saucer 113
sausage 87
saw 111
saxophone 159
scales 74
scallop 90
scanner 134
scarf 108
schoolbag 131
scissors 134
scoreboard 169
scourer 68
scratch card 101
screwdriver 110
screws 110
scrub 65
scrum 174
scuba diving 180
SD card 161
sea 155
sea bass 89
sea bream 89
seal 230
seashells 156
seaside 155
seatbelt 23
sea urchin 230
seaweed 156
security alarm 50
semi-detached house 47
Serrano ham 120
serving dish 58
sewing basket 166
sewing machine 166
shampoo 95
shark 230
sharpener 131
shaving foam 95
sheep 221
sheepdog 221
sheep's milk cheese 92
sheet music 160
sheets 61
shelves 53
shin 196
shin pads 173
shirt 106
shoe shop 112
shooting 190
shorts 106
shot put 187
shoulder 197
shower 63
shower gel 95
shower puff 62
showers 171
shower screen 63

showjumping 190
shrimp 90
shrub 66
shutter 50
shuttlecock 176
sideboard 53
sieve 56
SIGHTSEEING 144
sightseeing bus 31, 145
SIM card 128
singer 160
single room 151
sink 57, 63
sirloin steak 119
skate 89
skateboarding 190
SKELETON 198
skeleton 199
sketchpad 165
ski gloves 183
ski goggles 183
ski helmet 183
ski jacket 183
ski poles 183
skipping rope 171
skirt 107
skis 183
ski suit 183
skull 199
sledge 182
sleeping bag 153
sleepsuit 97
sliced bread 85
sliding doors 38
sling 210
slippers 108
slug 229
smartphone 128
smoke alarm 50
smoked cheese 92
snail 229
snake 223
snare drum 159
snooker 190
snorkel 156
snorkelling 180
snowboard 183
snowboarding boots 183
snow chains 29
snowsuit 97
soap 62, 95
soap dish 62
socks 107
sofa 53
soft furnishings 103
sole 195
sonographer 213
sorbet 121
soundbar 158
spade 65

Spanish omelette 120
spanner 110
spare wheel 29
sparkling water 76
sparrow 227
spatula 56
speakers 158
spectators 169
speed camera 26
speedometer 23
spices 75
spider 229
spinach 83
spine 199
spirit level 110
spirits 76
splinter 209
sponge 56
spoon 59
sports 165
sportsperson 169
spotlight 57
squash 176
squash ball 176
squash racket 176
squid 90
squirrel 224
stable 222
stadium 169
stall 78
stamp 101, 138
stands 169
stapler 134
starfish 230
stars 203
starting blocks 187
steak 87
steak knife 124
steering wheel 23
stepladder 110
stethoscope 201
sticky notes 134
sticky tape 134
sparkling water 76
sting 209
stitches 207
stopwatch 187
stork 227
strawberry 81
stream 235
streamers 239
street performer 244
student 131
studio flat 47
sugar 75
suitcase 41
sun 236
sunbathing 155
sunburn 209
sunflower 232
sunglasses 156
sunhat 156

suntan lotion 156
SUPERMARKET 73
surfboard 180
surfing 180
sushi 126
swallow 227
swan 227
sweatshirt 107
sweets 75
swimming cap 179
swimming pool 179
swimming trunks 156, 179
swimsuit 107, 156, 179
swivel chair 134
synagogue 140
syringe 191, 201
table 124
tablecloth 124
tablet 94, 128, 191
table tennis 190
taekwondo 185
tail 17, 217
talcum powder 98
tampon 95
tap 57, 63
tapas 148
tape measure 166
tea 116
teabags 75
team 169
teaspoon 59
tea towel 68
tee 188
teeth 203
teething ring 98
telephone 134
tennis 177
tennis ball 177
tennis court 177
tennis player 177
tennis racket 177
tent 141, 153
tent peg 141
textbook 131
thalassotherapy 215
theatre 148
thermometer 201
thermostat 50
thigh 196
Three Kings 243
(three-piece) suit 107
thumb 195
tibia 199
ticket 38
ticket barrier 38
ticket machine 38
ticket office 38
tie 107
tiger 225
tights 107
tilecutter 110

249

tiles 57, 110
till point 72
TIME 14
timetable 19
tin opener 56
toad 223
toast 116
tobacco 101
TOBACCONIST 100
toe 195
toenail 195
toilet 63
toilet brush 63
toiletries 151
toilet roll 63
toll point 26
tomato 83
toothbrush 95, 203
toothpaste 95, 203
toothpicks 124
torch 153
tortoise 223
tour guide 145
tourist office 145
towel rail 63
town hall 140
tow truck 29
toys 103
toyshop 112
track 38
track cycling 190
track shoes 187
trader 78

traditional Chinese
  medicine 215
traffic cone 26
traffic lights 26
traffic warden 26
train 38
trainers 108
train station 38
tram 38
travel agency 112
travel cot 99
travelling 143
trawler 44
treadmill 171
trellis 66
tripod 161
trolley 74
trombone 159
trophy 169
tropical fish 220
trousers 107
trout 89
trowel 65
trumpet 159
T-shirt 107
tuba 160
tumble drier 68
tumbler 59
tuna 89
tunnel 26
turkey 221
turntable 158
turtle 223
TV 53

TV stand 53
tweezers 210
twin room 151
tyre 22, 33
ulna 199
ultrasound 213
umbrella 7
umpire 177
umpire's chair 177
USB stick 134
vacuum cleaner 68
valley 235
vegetable oil 69, 75
vegetables 110
veloute 118
Venetian blind 53
vertebrae 199
vest 97
VET 216
villa 47
vinegar 75
vinegar and oil 124
violin 160
volcano 235
volleyball 190
vulture 227
waffle 85
waiter 124
waiting room 201
waitress 124
walking 143
wall light 53
wallpaper 110
ward 207

wardrobe 61
warning triangle 29
washing line 68
washing machine 68
wasp 229
watching TV/films
  143
watercolours 165
waterfall 235
watering can 65
watermelon 81
water polo 190
waterskiing 180
WATER SPORTS 178
waves 155
WEATHER 16
weedkiller 65
weightlifting 190
weightlifting bench
  171
WELLBEING 170
Wellington boots
  65
wetsuit 180
wet wipes 98
whale 230
wheel 33
wheelbarrow 65
wheelchair 207
whisk 57
whistle 177
white 7
whiteboard 131
willow 233

window 22, 45, 50
windowbox 65
windscreen 22
windscreen wiper 22
windsurfing 180
wine 76
wine glass 59, 124
wine shop 112
wing 22
wing mirror 22
WINTER SPORTS 181
wireless router 128
wok 57
wolf 224
wood-burning
  stove 50
wooden spoon 57
woodlouse 229
woodwork 164
woolly hat 108
WORK 12
worktop 57
wrap 116
wrench 110
wrestling 185
wrist 195
X-ray 207
xylophone 160
yacht 44
yellow 7
yellow card 173
yoghurt 91
zebra crossing 26
Zimmer frame® 207

SPANISH

abdomen 196
abeja 228
abeto 233
abrelatas 56
abrigo 105
acantilado 236
accesorios 49
aceite de oliva 75
aceite esencial 214
aceite vegetal 69,
  75
aceitunas 76, 120
acera 26
acordeón 158
acuarelas 165
acuario 222
acupuntura 214
adorno 53
aeropuerto 40
agencia de viajes 112
agencia
  inmobiliaria 111
agua con gas 76
agua sin gas 76
águila 226

aguja de ganchillo
  166
aguja y el hilo 166
agujas de hacer
  punto 166
airbag 29
aire acondicionado
  49
ajedrez 163
ajo 83
álamo 233
alargador 49
alarma contra
  incendios 50
alarma de seguridad
  50
albaricoque 80
alcachofa 82
aleta 22
aletas 156, 179
alfileres 166
alfombra 53, 61
alfombrilla de
  baño 62
alga marina 156

algodón 98
alicates 110
almeja 90
almendro 232
almohada 61
almohadilla 169
alondra 226
altavoces 158
altavoz de
  Bluetooth® 158
amapola 232
amarillo 7
amarradero 44
ampolla 209
anca 43
andador 99, 207
andén 37
ANFIBIOS Y REPTILES
  223
anguila 230
anillo de dentición
  98
ANIMALES
  DOMÉSTICOS 219
antena 50
anticongelante 29

antiséptico 94, 210
Año Nuevo chino 241
aparador 53, 57
apio 82
aplique de pared 53
arándano 80
araña 229
árbitra 169, 177
árbitro 169, 177
arbusto 66
archivador 133
arco iris 236
ardilla 224
área de juegos 140
área de penalti 167
arena 155
arenque 89
armario 61
armario de baño 63
armónica 159
arpa 159
arrecife de coral 236
arroyo 235
arroz 75, 118
arroz con leche 121

ARTESANÍAS 164
artículos de
  cocina 103
artículos de cuero
  103
artículos de
  perfumería 151
artista callejero 244
asa 113
aspiradora 68
astilla 209
atleta 186
ATLETISMO 186
atril 160
atún 89
auriculares 158
aurora 236
AUTOBÚS 30
autobús 31
autobús turístico 31,
  145
autocar 31
autocaravana 153
autopista 25
auxiliar sanitaria 201

auxiliar sanitario 201
AVES 226
avestruz 227
avión 40
avispa 229
ayuntamiento 140
azadón 65
azúcar 75
azúcar glas 74
azucena 232
azul 7
azulejos 57
babero 97
babosa 229
bacalao 89
bache 26
bádminton 176
bajante 50
bajo 158
balcón 45
baldosas 110
ballena 230
ballet 147
BALONCESTO 175
balonmano 189
bálsamo de labios 96
BANCA 135
banco de pesas 171
bandeja de entrada 133
bandeja de la arena 222
bandeja de salida 133
bandeja del horno 55
banderitas de colores 239
bañador 156, 179
bañera 63
bañera para bebé 99
BAÑO 62
baño 63
bar 123, 147
bar móvil 37
barbilla 195
barca de remos 44
barra de pan 84, 115
barra de sonido 158
base 96
bastoncillo 98
bastones de esquí 183
bata 106
batidora 57
batidora de mano 55
batidora manual 55
bebida con burbujas 76
bebidas alcohólicas 76
beicon 87
béisbol 189
Belén 243
berberecho 90

berenjena 82
biberón 98
biblioteca 131, 140
BICHOS PEQUEÑOS 228
BICICLETA 32
bicicleta 33
bicicleta elíptica 170
bicicleta estática 171
bidet 63
bikini 105, 155
billete 19
billetes de banco 72, 136
bistec 87
blanco 7
bloc de notas 133
bloque de apartamentos 47
bloque de oficinas 140
bloque de pisos 45
blusa 105
boca 195
bocadillo 126
body 97
bodyboarding 179
boda 243
bolígrafo 101, 130, 165
bollos 115
bolos 163
bolsa de golf 188
bolsa de papel 72
bolsa de plástico 72, 78
bolsa de viaje 41
bolsa reutilizable 72
bolsitas de té 75
bolso 108
bolso cambiador 98
bomba de bicicleta 33
bomba de pie 153
bombilla 49, 109
bombo 158
bordado 164
bordillo 25
bosque 234
bote inflable 44
botiquín de primeros auxilios 191, 193
botitas 97
botones 166
boutique 111

boya 43
bozal 222
bragas 106
brákets 203
brazo 196
brécol 82
bricolaje 143
brie 92
buceo con tubo 180
bufanda 108
buganvilla 231
búho 227
buitre 227
burro 221
buzón 51, 138
caballa 89
caballete 165
caballo 221
cabestrillo 210
cabeza 196
cabina 41
cabina del piloto 17, 41
cables de arranque 29
cabra 221
cabrales 92
cachipolla 229
cadena 33
cadenas para nieve 29
cadera 197
café 116
café con leche 113, 116
café instantáneo 74
cafetera 55
cafetería 131, 139
caimán 223
caja 72, 78, 138, 159
caja de bombones 239
caja de fusibles 49
caja fuerte 151
caja fuerte de seguridad 136
cajero automático 136
cajón 57
calabacín 82
calamar 90
calamares a la romana 127
calcetines 107
calculadora 133
caldera 49
caldo 118
calzado 103
calzoncillos 105
cama 61
cama de hospital 207
cámara 145

cámara compacta 161
cámara DSLR 161
cámara para casco 34
camarera 124
camarero 124
camarón 90
camello 225
caminar 143
camisa 106
camiseta 107
CAMPING 152
campo de fútbol 167, 173
campo de rugby 174
campus 131
canalón 50
canario 220
canasta 175
cancha de baloncesto 175
candado para la bicicleta 33
cangrejo 90, 230
cangrejo de río 90
canguro 225
cantante 160
capó 22
cápsula 94
cara 195, 196
caracol 229
carambola 81
caravana 153
cargador 128
CARNAVAL 244
carne picada 87
CARNICERÍA 86
carpeta 133
carpeta de anillas 134
carpintería 164
carrera automovilística 190
carrera de caballos 189
carrera de relevos 187
carrera de vallas 186
carreras de motociclismo 189
carretera 26
carretilla 65
carril 25
carrito de golf 188
carrito portaequipajes 41
carro 74
carroza de carnaval 244
carta 138
cartas 163

cartel de "no molestar" 150
cartera 138
cartero 138
CASA 48
casa 50
casa de cambio 136
casa de labranza 47
casa individual 47
casa pareada 47
cascada 235
casco 33, 34, 183, 184
caseta del perro 222
casino 147
casita para pájaros 66
castaño 232
castillo 145
castillo de arena 156
catedral 139, 145
cazo 56
cazuela 55
cebolla 83
celo 134
celosía 66
centro de conferencias 139
centro deportivo 169
cepillo 96
cepillo de dientes 95, 203
cerámica 164
cerdo 221
cereales 115
cereza 80
cerillas 153
cerveza 76
césped 66
cesta 69, 74, 78
cesta de la costura 166
cesta de la ropa sucia 60
cesta del pan 123
cesta del perro 222
chaleco reflectante 29
chaleco salvavidas 44, 184
chalet 47
champán 239
champiñón 83
champú 95
chanclas 155
chaqueta 106
chaqueta de cuero 34
chaqueta de esquí 183
chaqueta de punto 105
chile 82

251

chimenea 50, 53
chimpancé 225
chocolate 76
chocolate con churros 116, 126
chorizo 87
chuleta 87
chuletas de cordero 119
chupete 99
churros 84
ciclismo en pista 190
ciempiés 228
ciervo 224
cigarrillo 100
cigarrillo electrónico 100
cigarro 100
cigüeña 227
cincel 109
cine 147
cinta de correr 171
cinta métrica 166
cinturón 107
cinturón de seguridad 23
ciprés 232
circo 147
círculo central 167
ciruela 81
cisne 227
clarinete 158
clavel 231
clavícula 199
clavos 109
clientes 78
clip 134
cobaya 220
cobertizo 64
COCHE 20
coche 22
coche restaurante 38
cochecito 99
cochinilla 229
cocido madrileño 118
COCINA 54
cocina 57, 143
cocodrilo 223
codo 197
cojín 53
col 82
col de Bruselas 82
cola 17, 217
colchón 61
colchoneta inflable 153
coliflor 82
colina 235
colirio 205
collar 108, 222
collar antiparasitario 216
collarín 216

collarín cervical 210
colorete 96
columna vertebral 199
comadrona 213
COMEDOR 58
comerciante 78
COMER EN EL RESTAURANTE 122
cómic 100
comida de Navidad 243
comida para bebé 98
comida para mascotas 222
COMIDA RÁPIDA 125
comida y la bebida 103
COMIDAS PRINCIPALES 117
comisaría de policía 140
cómoda 61
compras 143
compresa 95
compresa de hielo 210
COMUNICACIÓN Y LA INFORMÁTICA 127
concesionario de automóviles 111
conchas 156
concierto 148
concursos de saltos 190
conejera 222
conejo 220
confeti 239
cono de tráfico 26
CONSULTA 200
CONSULTA DEL DENTISTA 202
contador 50
contrabajo 159
contraventana 50
copa alta 123
copa de cava 59
copa de vino 59
coral 230
corbata 107
cordero asado 119
coro 160
correr 143
cortacésped 65
corte 209
cortinas 52, 61
cosméticos 103
costa 236
costillar 87
costillas 199

cous cous 74, 118
crampones 182
cráneo 199
crema catalana 121
crema de pañal 98
CRIATURAS MARINAS 230
crisantemo 231
croissant 85, 116
cronómetro 187
croquetas 120
cruce 25
crucigrama 163
cuaderno 101
cuaderno de bocetos 165
cuaderno de ejercicios 130
cuadra 222
cuadrilátero de boxeo 184
cuadro 33, 53
cúbito 199
cubo 67
cubo de la basura 68
cubo de pedal 54
cubo y la pala 155
cucaracha 228
cuchara 59
cuchara de madera 57
cucharilla 59
cuchillo de cocina 56
cuchillo de pescado 124
cuchillo del queso 123
cuchillo para la carne 124
cuchillo y el tenedor 59
cuello 196
cuenco 57
cuenta 123
cuerda 182
cuerda de saltar 171
cuerda para tender 68
CUERPO 194
cuerpo 196, 197
cuervo 226
cueva 234
cuna 99
cuna de viaje 99
dados 163
damas 163
dardos 163
decoraciones 239
dedo 195
dedo del pie 195

dedo gordo del pie 195
delfín 230
delineador 96
dentadura postiza 203
dentífrico 95, 203
dentista 203
deportes 143
DEPORTES ACUÁTICOS 178
DEPORTES DE COMBATE 184
DEPORTES DE INVIERNO 181
DEPORTES DE RAQUETA 176
deportista 169
deportivas 108
DESAYUNO 115
desfile 244
desierto 234
desodorante 95
destornillador 110
Día de Todos los Santos 241
DÍAS, LOS MESES Y LAS ESTACIONES 15
dientes 203
director 160
directora 160
discoteca 148
disfraz 237, 244
Diwali 241
DJ 160
doble techo 141
dominó 163
donut 85
dorada 89
DORMITORIO 60
dormitorio 61
dron 161
ducha 63
duchas 171
ecografía 213
ecografista 213
edredón 61
edredón nórdico 61
EDUCACIÓN 129
Eid-al-Fitr 241
elefante 225
EMBARAZO 212
embutidos 118
emmental 92
empanada 85
encendido 23
encías 203
EN EL CENTRO 139
ENFERMEDAD 211
enfermera 193
enfermera dental 203

enfermero 193
enfermero dental 203
enjuague bucal 95, 203
ensalada 119
ensaladera 58
ensaladilla rusa 118
ENTRADA 51
entrada 50
equipo 169
erizo 224
erizo de mar 230
escalada 189
escalera de mano 110
escáner 134
escarabajo 228
escayola 207
escoba 67
escobilla del váter 63
escritorio 133
escuchar música 143
escurridor 55, 57
ESENCIAL 8, 18, 46, 70, 114, 142, 168, 192, 218, 238
esgrima 185
esmalte de uñas 96
espalda 197
espárrago 82
espátula 56
especias 75
espectáculo de humor 148
espectadores 169
espejo 61, 63
espinaca 83
espinilla 196
espinilleras 173
esponja 63
esponja de malla 62
espuma de afeitar 95
ESQUELETO 199
esqueleto 199
esquí acuático 180
esquís 183
estaca 141
estación de peaje 26
estación de tren 38
estadio 169
ESTANCO 100
estanque 235
estantería 53
esterilla 183
esternón 199
estetoscopio 201
estofado de lentejas 118
estrella de mar 230
estrellas 236
estropajo 68
estuche 131

estuche de gafas 205
estuche de las lentillas 205
estudiante 131
estudio 47
estufa de leña 50
examen ocular 205
fabada 119
fabricación de joyas 164
falda 107
Fallas 241
FAMILIA Y LOS AMIGOS 10
farmacéutica 193
farmacéutico 193
FARMACIA 93
farmacia 193
faro 22
fémur 199
feria 147, 148, 239
ferry 44
fichas 163
fideos chinos 118, 126
fiesta 239
FIESTAS 240
figura de carnaval 244
filete 87, 119
film transparente 54
fitoterapia 214
flamenco 226
flan 121
flauta 159
flor de pascua 232
flores 66
FLORES, LAS PLANTAS Y LOS ÁRBOLES 231
floristería 111
flotador 156
foca 230
foco 57
fórmula 98
fotocopiadora 134
FOTOGRAFÍA 161
fractura 209
frambuesa 81
fregona 68
freidora 55
freno 33
freno de mano 23
frente 195
fresa 81
frigorífico combi 57
FRUTAS Y VERDURAS 79
frutera 62
frutos secos 76
fuegos artificiales 243
fuente 140
fuente de servir 58

FÚTBOL 172
fútbol americano 189
gafas 205
gafas de esquí 183
gafas de natación 179
gafas de sol 156
galletas 74
gamba 90
gambas al ajillo 120
garaje 29, 50
garza 226
garra 217
gasa 210
gasolinera 26
gatera 222
gato 29, 220
gaviota 226
gazpacho 119
geco 223
gel de ducha 95
geranio 231
gimnasia 189
girasol 232
glaciar 234
gofre 85
GOLF 188
golondrina 227
golosinas 76
goma de borrar 130
gorila 225
gorra de béisbol 107
gorra de lana 108
gorrión 227
gorro 179
gotas 94
goteo 207
gradas 169
GRANDES ALMACENES 102
grapadora 134
grifo 57, 63
grillo 228
grosella roja 81
grúa 29
grulla 226
grupo de acompañamiento 160
guantera 23
guantes 108
guantes de boxeo 184
guantes de cuero 34
guantes de esquí 183
guantes de goma 68
guantes de jardinería 64
guantes de portero 173
guardia de tráfico 26
guía 145

guía turística 145
guisante 83
guitarra acústica 158
guitarra eléctrica 159
habitación de dos camas 151
habitación doble 150
habitación individual 151
halcón 226
halterofilia 190
hamburguesa 87, 126
hámster 220
hastial 50
helado 121
helicóptero 17
herbicida 65
herbolario 112
hiedra 233
hierbas 74
hilo dental 203
hipnoterapia 214
hipopótamo 225
hockey 189
hockey sobre hielo 189
hogaza de pan 85
hojas de partitura 160
Holi 241
hombro 197
homeopatía 214
hongo 233
HORA 14
horario 19
hormiga 228
hornillo de gas 153
horno 57
horno microondas 57
horquilla de jardín 64
HOSPITAL 206
hospital 140, 193
HOTEL 149
hotel 140
huevo 91
húmero 199

iglesia 139
iguana 223
iluminación 103
imperdible 166
impresora 134
incubadora 213
indicador de la gasolina 23
interfono 51
intermitente 22
iris 232
isla 236

jabalí 224
jabalina 186

jabón 62, 95
jabonera 62
jacinto 232
jamón 87
jamón serrano 120
Janucá 241
jarabe para la tos 94
JARDÍN 64
jardín 66
jardinera 65
jardinería 143
jardines 145
jarra de agua 124
jarra medidora 56
jaula 222
jefa de tren 37
jefe de tren 37
jeringuilla 191, 201
jirafa 225
joyería 112
judías estofadas 118
judías verdes 83
juego de mesa 163
JUEGOS 162
juez de línea 173, 177
jugador de baloncesto 175
jugador de fútbol 173
jugador de rugby 174
jugadora de baloncesto 175
jugadora de fútbol 173
jugadora de rugby 174
juguetería 112
juguetes 103
juzgado 139

kárate 185
kayak 44, 180
ketchup 74
kickboxing 185
kiwi 80
kung fu 185

LABORES DE LA CASA 67
laca para el pelo 96
lagarto 223
lago 235
lámpara de escritorio 133
lámpara de mesilla de noche 51
langosta 90, 230
lanzamiento de disco 186
lanzamiento de peso 187
lápiz 101, 130, 165
laurel 233
lavabo 57, 63
lavachoches 25
lavadora 68

lavandería 140
lavavajillas 67
leche 91
leche frita 121
lechuga 83
lector de tarjetas 72
lectura 143
lencería 103
lentejas 74
lentillas 205
león 225
leotardos 107
LESIONES 208
libélula 228
librería 52, 111
libro de texto 131
liebre 224
lienzo 165
limón 80
limpiaparabrisas 22
linterna 153
litera 37
llave de tarjeta 151
llave inglesa 110
lobo 224
loción bronceadora 94, 156
loción para bebé 98
lombriz 229
loro 217, 220
lubina 89
luces navideñas 243
lucha libre 185
luna 236
luz delantera 33

maceta 65, 66
magdalena 85, 116
magulladura 209
malecón 43
maleta 41
maletero 22
mallas 106
MAMÍFEROS 224
mampara de la ducha 63
manchego 92
mancuernas 170
mandíbula 195
mando a distancia 52
mango 80
manguera 64
manguitos 179
manillar 33
mano 195, 196
manoplas 97
manta 60
mantel 124
mantequilla 91
manualidades de papel 164
manzana 80
mapa 19, 101

253

mapa de la ciudad 145
máquina de coser 166
máquina de remo 171
máquina expendedora de billetes 38
mar 155
maracuyá 81
marcador 169
marchas 33
margarina 91
margarita 231
mariposa 228
mariquita 229
marisma 235
marquesina 31
martillo 109
martín pescador 226
masaje 215
máscara 237, 244
máscara de oxígeno 207
máscara y el tubo de buceo 156
matrícula 22
mayonesa 75
mecánica 29
mecánico 29
medalla 169
médica 193
médica de familia 201
medicina 94, 193
medicina tradicional china 215
médico 193
médico de familia 201
meditación 215
medusa 230
mejilla 195
mejillón 90
mejillones 120
melé 174
melocotón 81
melón 80
memoria USB 134
menú 124
mercadillo navideño 243
MERCADO 77
merengue 121
merluza 83
merluza en salsa verde 119
mermelada 74, 116
mermelada de naranja 75
mesa 124
mesa de centro 53

mesa de exploración 201
mesa de la tele 53
mesilla de noche 61
meta 167, 173
metro 37
mezquita 140
microbús 31
miel 74
milhoja 85
minibar 151
mirlo 226
mobiliario 103
mochila escolar 131
mochila 153
moda 103
modelismo 164
moisés 99
molinillo de pimienta 58
molinillo de sal 58
monedas 72
monitor 207
mono 97, 225
montaña 235
monte bajo 235
montura 205
monumento 145
mora 81
morro 17
mosca 229
mosquito 229
mostrador de facturación 41
MOTO 34
moto 34
moto de agua 179
mousse de chocolate 121
móvil 99
moza 151
mozo 151
mozzarella 92
mueble vitrina 52
muebles de jardín 66
muesli 116
muletas 207
muñeca 195
murciélago 224
museo 145
museo de arte 145
musgo 233
MÚSICA 157
música 160
musical 148
músico 160
muslo 196
nalgas 197
naranja 81
narciso 231
nariz 195
nata 91
natillas 121

NAVIDAD Y EL AÑO NUEVO 242
negro 7
netball 190
neumático 22, 33
nevera de camping 153
nivel de burbuja 110
notas adhesivas 134
nubes 236
nudillo 195
nutria 224
objetivo de la cámara 161
oca 221
oculista 112, 205
oficial 169
OFICINA 132
OFICINA DE CORREOS 137
oficina de turismo 145
ojo 195
olas 155
olivo 233
olla exprés 56
ópera 148
ÓPTICA 204
orca 230
ordenador 128
ordenador portátil 133
oreja 195
orquesta 160
orquídea 232
oruga 228
oso 225
osteopatía 215
ostra 90
OTRAS TIENDAS 111
OTROS DEPORTES 189
oveja 221
ovillo de lana 166
pacientes 193
paella 119
paellera 56
pala 65
palanca de marchas 23
paleta 17, 65, 165
palillos de dientes 124
palma 195
palo de golf 188
paloma 226, 227
palomitas 76
pan 69
PANADERÍA-PASTELERÍA 84
pan con tomate 115
pan de molde 85
panecillos 84, 115
panera 54

paño de cocina 68
pantalla de información 37, 41
pantalón 107
pantalón corto 106
pantalones de chándal 106
pantorrilla 197
pañal 98
paño de cocina 68
Papá Noel 243
papaya 81
papel 130, 165
papel de aluminio 55
papel de cocina 54
papel pintado 110
paquete 138
PARA BEBÉ 97
parabrisas 22
parachoques 22
parada de autobús 31
paraguas 7
paramédica 193
paramédico 193
parasol 65
parchís 163
parking 25
parmesano 92
parque 140
parque de bomberos 139
parquímetro 25
parra 233
partido de baloncesto 175
partido de fútbol 173
pasaporte 41
pasarela 43
Pascua 241
paseo marítimo 156
pasillo 150
paso a nivel 25
paso de cebra 26
pasta 75, 118
pastel de hojaldre 85
pasteles 95
pastilla 94, 191
pastillas para la garganta 94
pastizal 235
patata 83
patatas 118
patatas bravas 120
patatas fritas 76, 126
patinaje en monopatín 190
patinaje sobre hielo 182
patines de hielo 182
patio 66
pato 221
pavo 221
pavo real 227

pececito rojo 220
peces tropicales 220
pecho 196
pechuga de pollo 87
pedal 33
pelador 56
peine 96
pelele 97
pelícano 227
pelo 195
pelota de baloncesto 175
pelota de fútbol 173
pelota de golf 188
pelota de playa 155
pelota de rugby 174
pelota de squash 176
pelota de tenis 177
pelota suiza 171
peluquería 111, 112
pelvis 199
pendientes 108
península 236
pensamiento 232
pepino 83
pera 81
percha 60
periódico 101
periquito 220
peroné 199
perrito caliente 126
perro 220
perro pastor 221
persiana 53
pesa rusa 171
pesca 189
pescado frito 119
pesquero de arrastre 44
petanca 190
petirrojo 227
petisú 85
peto 106
peto de esquí 183
piano 159
picadura 209
pico 217
pie 195, 196
pierna 196
pieza de carne para asar 87
pijama 106
piloto 41
pimienta 75
pimiento rojo 83
pincel 109, 165
pincho 126
pingüino 227
pino 233
pintalabios 96
pintura 109

pintura al óleo 165
pintura facial 244
pinturas 130
pinzas 210
pinzas de la ropa 67
pinzón 226
piña 81
piolet 182
piragua 44
piragüismo 179
piscina 179
pista 183
pista de aterrizaje 41
pista de atletismo 187
pista de tenis 177
pisto 119
pizarra 131
pizza 126
plancha 68
planta 195
plátano 69, 80, 233
platillo 113
platillos 159
plato 59, 158
PLAYA 154
playa 155
plaza 78
plaza de aparcamiento 25
plaza de aparcamiento accesible 25
pluma 237
podio 169
polilla 229
pollo 221
pollo asado 118
polvo facial 96
polvos de talco 98
pomada 210
pomelo 80
poni 220
POR LA NOCHE 146
porta mascotas 216
portabebés 99
portaequipajes 37
portera 173
portero 173
postal 101, 138
poste SOS 29
postes de rugby 174
poza de marea 236
preservativo 94
primeros auxilios 210
PROBLEMAS CON EL COCHE 27
productos 78
productos de confitería 100
profesor universitario 131

profesora universitaria 131
protector bucal 184
puente 25
puerro 83
puerta 22, 50, 66
puerta principal 50
puertas corredizas 38
puerto 43, 44
puesto 78
pulgar 195
pulpo 90
pulpo a la gallega 120
pulsera 107
puntos 207
puré de verdura 118
putter 188
puzzle 163
quemador 57
quemadura 209
quemadura del sol 209
queso ahumado 92
queso cheddar 92
queso de cabra 92
queso de mahón 92
QUESO Y LOS LÁCTEOS 91
quirófano 207
quiropráctica 214
radar de velocidad 26
radiador 50
radio 52, 199
radio despertador 60
radiografía 207
rallador 55
Ramadán 241
ramo de flores 239
rana 223
rape 89
raqueta de bádminton 176
raqueta de squash 176
raqueta de tenis 177
rata 224
ratón 224
raya 89
recepción 151
recepcionista 151
recipiente para mezclar 56
recogedor 68
recogepelotas 177
recogida de equipajes 40
reflector 33
reflexología 215
regadera 65
regalo 239
regla 131
remo de kayak 180

remolacha 82
remos 180
repelente de insectos 94
reposacabezas 23
reposapiés 53
reproductor de Blue-ray® 52
reproductor de DVD 52
requesón 92
restaurante 148
retrovisor 23
retrovisor lateral 22
revista 101
revista de rompecabezas 101
Reyes Magos 243
rímel 96
rinoceronte 225
río 235
roble 233
robot de cocina 55
rocas 235
rodilla 196
rodillo de cocina 56
rodillo de pintura 110
rojo 7
rollo de papel higiénico 63
ROPA Y EL CALZADO 104
rosa 232
Roscón de Reyes 243
rotonda 26
rotor 17
rótula 199
router inalámbrico 128
rozadura 209
rueda 22, 33
rueda de recambio 29
RUGBY 174
rugby 174
sábanas 61
sacacorchos 55
sacapuntas 131
saco de boxeo 184
saco de dormir 153
sal 75
sala de conferencias 131
sala de espera 201
sala de hospital 207
sala de parto 213
sala de reconocimiento 201
salamandra 223
salchicha 87
salmón 89
SALÓN 52

salón 53
salón de belleza 111
salpicadero 23
salsera 58
saltamontes 229
salto con pértiga 187
salto de altura 186
salto de longitud 186
SALUD Y BIENESTAR 11
salvavidas 43
sal y la pimienta 124
sandalias 108
sandía 81
sándwich 126
sanfermines 241
Santa Claus 243
sapo 223
sardina 89
sartén 55
sauce 233
saxofón 159
secador de pelo 60
secadora 68
sello 101, 138
semáforo 26
Semana Santa 241
sendero 66
serpentines 239
serpiente 223
servilleta 58, 124
sierra 110
sierra de arco 109
silbato 173
silla 123
silla del árbitro 177
silla del dentista 203
silla de montar 33
silla de ruedas 207
silla giratoria 134
sillita 99
sillita de coche para niño 99
sillón 53, 61
sinagoga 140
sistema de navegación 23
snooker 190
sobre 100, 138
sobre acolchado 138
SOBRE TI 9
socorrista 179
sofá 53
sol 236
sombra de ojos 96
sombrero para el sol 156
sombrilla 155
sorbete 121
squash 176
stand up 180
suavizante 95
submarinismo 180
sudadera 107

suelo impermeable 141
suéter 106
sujetador 105
SUPERMERCADO 73
surfing 180
surtidor de gasolina 25
sushi 126
tabaco 101
tabla de cortar 55
tabla de planchar 68
tabla de snowboard 183
tabla de surf 180
tabla optométrica 205
tableta 128
tacos de salida 187
taekwondo 185
taladradora 133
taladro eléctrico 109
talasoterapia 215
talón 195
tamiz 56
tampón 95
tapas 148
taquilla 38, 171
tarima 64
tarjeta amarilla 173
tarjeta de crédito 72, 136
tarjeta de débito 72, 136
tarjeta de embarque 41
tarjeta de felicitación 101, 239
tarjeta de memoria 161
tarjeta de rasque y gane 101
tarjeta roja 173
teclado 159
tarjeta SIM 128
tarta 239
tarta de chocolate 121
tarta de queso 121
tarta de Santiago 121
tartaleta de fruta 85
taza 113
taza y platillo 59
té 116
teatro 148
tee 188
tejado 22, 45, 50
tejón 224
tela 166
telas para cortinas y tapicerías 103
tele 53
teléfono 134

255

teléfono inteligente 128
tendedero 67
tenis 177
tenis de mesa 190
tenista 177
tensiómetro 201
TERAPIAS ALTERNATIVAS 214
termómetro 201
termostato 50
test de embarazo 213
tibia 199
tiburón 230
TIEMPO 16
tienda 141
tienda de antigüedades 111
tienda de artículos para regalo 112
TIENDA DE BRICOLAJE 109
tienda de campaña 141, 153
tienda de electrodomésticos 111
tienda de mascotas 112
tienda de muebles 111
tienda de música 112
tienda de playa 155
tienda de telefonía móvil 112
tienda de vinos 112
tienda libre de impuestos 41
tienda solidaria de segunda mano 111
tierra de cultivo 234
TIERRA, EL MAR Y EL CIELO 234
tigre 225
tijeras 134
tijeras de poda 65
tijeras de tela 166
timbre 33, 51
tinta 165
tipo de cambio 136
tique de compra 72
tirita 94, 191, 210
tiro 190
tiro al arco 189
toalla de baño 62
toalla de mano 62
toalla de playa 155
toallero 63
toallitas húmedas 98
tobillo 195
tocado 244
tocador 60
toldo 64
tomate 83
Tomatina de Buñol 241
topo 224
tornillos tirafondos 110
tornillos y tuercas 109
torno 38
torno del dentista 203
toro 221
torta del casar 92
tortilla 126
tortilla de patatas 120
tortitas 85
tortuga 223
tortuga de tierra 223
tostada 116
TRABAJO 12
tráilla 222
trampolín 179
transatlántico 44
TRANSPORTE EN TREN 35
tranvía 38
trapo 67
tren 38
tren ligero 37
triángulo de emergencia 29
trineo 182
trípode 161
tritón 223
trofeo 169
trombón 159
trompeta 159
trona 67
trucha 89
tuba 160
tubo superior del cuadro 33
tumbona 155
túnel 26
TURISMO 144
uña 195
uña del pie 195
uva 80
vaca 221
vagón 37
valla 66
valle 235
vaqueros 106
vaso 59
vaso de vino 124
váter 63
velero 44
velocímetro 23
vendaje 94, 191, 210
ventana 45, 50
ventanilla 22
ventilador de techo 49
ver la tele 143
ver películas 143
verde 7
verduras 119
vértebras 199
vestido 106
vestuarios 170
VETERINARIO 216
vía de tren 38
viajar 143
VIAJES EN AVIÓN 39
VIAJES EN BARCO 42
videojuegos 143
vieira 90
viento 141
vinagre 75
vinagre y aceite 124
vino 76
violín 160
violoncelo 158
visillos 61
vivero 111
volante 23, 176
volcán 235
vóleibol 190
waterpolo 190
windsurf 180
wok 57
wrap 126
xilófono 160
yate 44
yogurt 91
yudo 185
zanahoria 82
zapatería 112
zapatillas 108
zapatillas de baloncesto 175
zapatillas de boxeo 184
zapatillas para pista de atletismo 187
zapatos con cordones 108
zapatos de tacón alto 108
zorro 224
zumo de frutas 76
zumo de naranja 116

PHOTO CREDITS

Shutterstock: p19 timetable (Brendan Howard), p22 windscreen (JazzBoo), p31 minibus (Iakov Filimonov), p31 sightseeing bus (Roman Sigaev), p37 light railway (Bikeworldtravel), p37 refreshments trolley (Vassamon Anansuksakem), p38 ticket machine (Balakate), p38 ticket office (Michael715), p38 tram (smereka), p100 confectionery (Bitkiz), p103 cosmetics (mandritoiu), p103 food and drink (1000 words), p103 footwear (Toshio Chan), p103 kitchenware (NikomMaelao Production), p103 toys (Zety Akhzar), p111 electrical store (BestPhotoPlus), p111 estate agents (Barry Barnes), p112 gift shop (Pamela Loreto Perez), p112 pet shop (BestPhotoPlus), p136 bureau de change (Lloyd Carr), p138 postbox (Alexandros Michailidis), p139 church (Ilya Images), p139 conference centre (lou armor), p145 sightseeing bus (Roman Sigaev), p147 carnival (Tory studio), p147 casino (Benny Marty), p148 comedy show (stock_photo_world), p148 musical (Igor Bulgarin), p148 opera (criben), p156 promenade (Oscar Johns), p160 choir (Marco Saroldi), p160 orchestra (Ferenc Szelepcsenyi), p173 pitch (Christian Bertrand), p175 basketball shoes (Milos Vucicevic), p177 line judge (Leonard Zhukovsky), p177 umpire (Stuart Slavicky), p189 handball (Dziurek), p190 motor racing (Cristiano barni), p190 table tennis (Stefan Holm), p190 velodrome (Pavel L Photo and Video), p190 water polo (katacarix), p213 labour suite (ChameleonsEye), p241 Buñol Tomatina (Iakov Filimonov), p241 Running of the Bulls (imagestockdesign), p243 the Three Kings (zummolo), p244 costume (Melodia plus photos), p244 headdress (LongJon), p244 parade (Capricorn Studio), p244 street performer (Kizel Cotiw-an). All other images from Shutterstock.